PLATO AND TRADITION

SERIES EDITOR

John Russon

REREADING ANCIENT PHILOSOPHY

PLATO
AND
TRADITION

The Poetic and Cultural Context of Philosophy

PATRICIA FAGAN

 NORTHWESTERN UNIVERSITY PRESS • EVANSTON, ILLINOIS

Northwestern University Press
www.nupress.northwestern.edu

Printed in the United States of America

10 9 8 7 6 5 4 3 2 1

Library of Congress Cataloging-in-Publication Data
Fagan, Patricia, 1964–
    Plato and tradition: the poetic and cultural context of
philosophy / Patricia Fagan.
      p. cm.
    Includes bibliographical references and index.
    ISBN 978-0-8101-2864-4 (pbk.: alk. paper)
    1. Plato—Criticism and interpretation. 2. Plato. Dialogues.
Selections. 3. Socrates. I. Title.
B395.F255 2013
184—dc23
                                            2012028106

For John Russon

Without whom not

"Why, the truth is, my dear," said Mr. Pecksniff, smiling upon his assembled kindred, "that I am at a loss for a word. The name of those fabulous animals (pagan, I regret to say) who used to sing in the water, has quite escaped me."

Mr. George Chuzzlewit suggested, "Swans."

"No," said Mr. Pecksniff. "Not swans. Very like swans, too. Thank you."

The nephew with the outline of a countenance, speaking for the first and last time on that occasion, propounded, "Oysters."

"No," said Mr. Pecksniff, with his own peculiar urbanity, "nor oysters. But by no means unlike oysters; a very excellent idea; thank you, my dear sir, very much. Wait! Sirens. Dear me! Sirens, of course. I think, I say, that means might be devised of disposing our respected relative to listen to the promptings of nature, and not to the siren-like delusions of art."

—CHARLES DICKENS, *MARTIN CHUZZLEWIT*

CONTENTS

ACKNOWLEDGMENTS

This book has been in the making for a number of years. I have had the good fortune to be able to present versions of each of the first five chapters to audiences at a variety of universities; in every case I have been grateful for the helpful and stimulating responses to my work. So I offer my thanks to the philosophy departments of the University of Maine, the University of Kentucky, Northern Arizona University, the University of Guelph, and Galatasaray University in Istanbul, and to the Department of Classical Studies at the University of Western Ontario. Much of the thinking involved in this book has grown up while I taught courses in Greek history, culture, and literature at the University of Windsor, so I offer very special thanks to the students who have been the first sounding board for these ideas and arguments. I thank the Department of Languages, Literatures and Cultures at the University of Windsor and the university itself for providing me the resources necessary to pursue this work. Further, I thank the offices of the Dean of the Faculty of Arts and Social Sciences and of the Vice-President of Research for funds to support the publication of this book. I am grateful to Northwestern University Press and to Indiana University Press for permission to reprint chapters 4 and 5. The editors at Northwestern University Press were capable and helpful and collegial through every stage of the process of bringing this book to publication, so I offer them all my respect and gratitude. In particular I want to thank, for a variety of forms of care, challenge, and assistance, Jeffrey Banks, Meaghan Biddle, Susan Bredlau, Jesse Courtland, Mary deBruyn, John Fagan, Shirley Fagan, Kirsten Jacobson, Alexander Leferman, Sean Marzec, Max Nelson, Greg Recco, Eric Sanday, Lazaros Simeon, Christos Strubakos, Michal Tellos, Juanita Wattam, Kaitlyn Webster, and Robert Weir. Finally, I have dedicated this book to John Russon in acknowledgment of the key place he holds, as my dear friend and teacher, in the genesis and growth of this book and, more importantly, in my education and my growing up into the world.

Plato's dialogues occupy a unique place within the European and North American intellectual traditions. These texts, more than any others, are regarded as essential to understanding what it is that human beings are doing when they do philosophy. My own introduction to the study of philosophy at the university level began with the *Apology*. So it is and was for most of us who studied and study philosophy within postsecondary educational institutions.

Many people who are not professional academics or university students also look to Plato when they want to read philosophy. We turn to Plato for many reasons. Much of the appeal of these texts surely resides in the glorious figure of Socrates, whose wit and wickedness, humility and persistence draw us in with a kind of marveling breathlessness. In Socrates we see someone who opens our eyes to the profoundly serious nature of the philosophical enterprise. He is, after all, as Plato puts before us so vividly, a man who died for doing philosophy. The questions he pursues with his interlocutors are, many of them, dangerous questions: In a democracy, how can a city be well run when it is run by a group of people who do not appear competent to rule? How do we know that the actions we justify by claiming to do them in the name of the gods are in fact godly? Should we educate our young people to succeed in the eyes of their fellows or to be decent human beings? We read Plato and take Plato seriously because in his works we see the power and importance of the ideas philosophy raises and the questions philosophy asks.

What makes us see the power and importance of philosophy in Plato's texts is that they are not just philosophical argumentation—they are works of literary *art*. They are, as people have noted, dramas with fully fleshed-out characters embedded in a rich, complex world, with plots and conflicts, with humor, with evocative and subtle and sophisticated poetic language. To read Plato is to feel the challenge to the intellect as one tries to grasp the arguments, to strive toward the abstract universal truth. It is also to feel the *life* of those ideas, of those truths, as they are worked out in concrete, particular human situations in the drama. To read Plato is also to come to see how these ideas and truths are not just *Plato's* ideas and truths: they are the ideas and truths of Plato's world and of Plato's own heritage and traditions. The philosophical arguments are not separate from the poetic art, which is itself not separate from Plato's culture.

Plato's texts are larded with quotations from the poets, especially from the Homeric poems. Plato appeals regularly to the material of his own intellectual and artistic world, material well known and familiar to him and to his earliest readers. The characters in his dialogues are almost all real people who lived and breathed and walked the streets of Athens in the fifth century B.C.E. They are people about whom everyone—at least everyone in Athens—knew something. Gorgias came to Athens to teach. Agathon was a successful tragic poet. Alcibiades was—Alcibiades. The dialogues have, by and large, concrete settings with histories, meanings, and associations. The *Republic* takes place in the house of Cephalus in Peiraieus, where most of the Athenian metics lived because Peiraieus was developed in the fifth century to be Athens's port and center of trade. The *Crito* takes place in the Athenian jail near the agora, close to the law courts where Socrates was condemned. The dialogues take place at particular times, often with specific religious or political associations and significance. The *Symposium* takes place immediately following Agathon's first victory in the dramatic competitions at the Lenaea in 416 B.C.E., which is also the year in which the Athenians decided to send their great fleet, under the command of Alcibiades, Lamachus, and Nicias, to Sicily, with disastrous results. The *Republic* takes place at the time of the first celebration of the festival of the Thracian god Bendis in Peiraieus, probably around 411, evoking the associations of Peiraieus with non-Athenians and reminding the reader of Athenian openness to innovation, even in religion.

Opening up one of the dialogues, then, is opening up a door on Athens, on her poetry, her gods, her people, her places, her struggles. Plato draws us into that world as he draws that world into his philosophical argumentation. In *Republic,* the evocation of religious innovation with which the dialogue begins provides the setting for a discussion of far more profound innovations in politics, religion, and education. In *Symposium,* Agathon's victory at a festival in honor of Dionysus is the setting for speeches in honor of another god, Eros, which are interrupted by something like an epiphany of Dionysus when the drunken Alcibiades and his attendant revelers burst into Agathon's house to reveal the truth of Socrates's own eros. Fully to grasp Plato's philosophical points in these dialogues demands that we keep in mind the presence of these events and these places. Although we may want to read Plato as though all he writes is the philosophical argumentation, that is precisely what he does not do. The dialogues enact the ideas of the argumentation, adding to it through what is not always explicitly stated. Plato writes a world—his world—writes philosophy as an element in that world, and demands that we read his culture as well as his philosophy.

In this book, I am trying to live up to the demand that I read Plato's world. My contention is that if we read Plato's dialogues without seriously attending to the world that informs them and to the moments at which Plato draws our attention to that world, we are not reading Plato thoroughly enough and may, often, not see what Plato is doing and what Plato may well be telling us. So, for example, as I argue in my discussion of *Republic* 3 in chapter 3, when we read the *Republic*, the fact that Socrates says that traditional Greek poetry should not be included in the education of the new city should not lead us to think that *Plato* thinks that traditional Greek poetry should not be part of education. Indeed, when we carefully read Plato's accounts of myth and poetry in *Republic* 2 and 3 we discover that Plato provides us with a thoroughgoing analysis of each myth and poem he invokes and that his analysis and his choice of material for discussion have to lead us to question the value of Socrates's claim.

When we read Plato, then, and come across invocations of Plato's world, we should ask ourselves, what is going on here? To answer that question, we must then turn away from Plato's text and to his world. We should, if the remains of Greek culture allow it, explore the contexts out of which his quotations of poets and philosophers, his references to myth and religion, and his invocations of assumed social values all come. These explorations should keep in mind the fact that Plato's world made Plato and that these references to the world are not simply ornamental but deeply evocative of large systems of meaning for Plato and his earliest readers. Consequently, we should expect to find Plato's invocations of particular texts or events or practices invoking those structures of meaning as well. We should expect to see Plato manifesting a version of traditional referentiality, the invoking of immanent traditional meaning through the use of traditional diction, stories, and the like. Having performed this exploration, we can return to Plato's text knowing and understanding more of what Plato knew and understood. With this new knowledge and understanding, we are then in a position to begin to see the work that these references to the world are doing within their particular Platonic contexts.

In this book, I offer studies of six of Plato's dialogues, each of which attempts to address the question of what work some of Plato's references to the world are doing in each dialogue. I by no means claim to give a complete or even a thorough account of Plato's taking up of elements of his world and his cultural heritage in these dialogues. Rather, I have, in each study, focused my attention on one aspect of his cultural heritage that has seemed to me especially rich in the dialogue. I have arranged these studies under the rubrics of three themes: eros, the polis, and philosophy. Part I, "Eros and Tradition," studies two Platonic dialogues that focus on the nature of erotic love. Chapter 1 examines Plato's use of the ideal norms of the Classical Athenian pederastic relationship in Socrates's persuading Alcibiades to accept him as his lover in *Alcibiades* I. Here I argue that, despite Socrates's claims that he is *not* a typical Athenian lover, he nonetheless behaves toward Alcibiades in a way that is recognizably the behavior of an Athenian *erastēs* (adult male lover). Plato reworks the terms of that relationship, however, to open the way toward a new arena for eros; eros will be directed now toward the pursuit of *aretē*, and it will be worked out in a new, *philosophical* arena that will exist outside of the traditional homes of eros: the household and the polis. Chapter 2 works with Diotima's account of eros from the *Symposium*. I begin here by looking to Sappho to provide an account of eros against which to read Diotima. Here we see that Sappho and Diotima both provide an account of eros that sees it as part of reciprocal attitudes of care on the parts of lover and beloved. Diotima's eros, however, pushes itself beyond the relationship of lover and beloved to become care for the creation of laws and tradition. The wildness of eros that we see in Sappho's poems (its compulsive force) becomes in Diotima's eros the very thing that perpetuates tradition as it reveals itself to be the force that keeps people attached to their tradition through an insistence that what is traditional continue to be meaningful to them.

Part II, "Polis and Tradition," contains chapters on *Republic* 3 and on *Laws* 4. In chapter 3 I argue that Socrates's account of the effects of music in *Republic* 3 alludes heavily to the description of the Sirens in the *Odyssey*. These Sirens are destructive of human beings and human endeavors because they are, as the poem indicates, singers without tradition. In light of Socrates's evocation of the Sirens and the dangers of song without tradition, I examine Socrates's accounts of the kinds of stories that the songs in the new city will tell. These new stories will not be the traditional stories. Consequently, the citizens in the new city will not be educated in the kinds of values that cities rely upon, particularly *philia*. The city without tradition emerges as a city that will necessarily bring about its own destruction. In a similar vein, chapter 4 discusses the Athenian Stranger's analysis of the isolated location of the new city-foundation on Crete in light of the reference to the *Odyssey*'s Cyclopes in the history of political constitutions in *Laws* 3. As with the material in *Republic* 3, so here the poetic material invoked carries a meaning that is at odds with the stated claims of the Athenian Stranger, who insists on the *aretē* and freedom that will accrue to the citizens of the new foundation because of their city's isolation. In particular, the similarities between the isolated

Cyclopes and the isolated new city indicate that the new city will be a failure, unable to cope with the new or the strange except by destroying it.

Part III, "Philosophy and Tradition," takes up the *Apology* and the *Crito.* In chapter 5 I argue that Socrates, in his account of his quest to understand the oracle from Delphi that no one is wiser than Socrates, likens himself to the Athenian version of Oedipus. Plato uses the familiar Athenian story of a polluted kin-killer who is taken in by Athens and made one of their honored beneficent cult heroes to give the lie to Athens's regular portrayal of itself as open and tolerant. The Athenian Oedipus, Socrates, is rejected and killed by the Athenians as dangerous and offensive because of his philosophical life. Finally, in chapter 6, I discuss Socrates's conversation with Crito in the *Crito* in light of the themes of dishonor and abandonment of the heroic project evoked by Socrates's account of his dream, in which he implicitly compares himself to Achilleus. Here I argue that Plato models Crito on Thersites, from *Iliad* 2, showing that his urging of Socrates to flee his prison is tantamount to a recommendation to abandon a heroic project that helps to define Greek culture and self-identity: the Trojan War. The heroic Socrates, however, though dying in defense of his philosophical project of questioning tradition, reveals himself as critically aware of the importance of tradition and fully committed to the protection of Athens and her laws.

Through these studies, I hope to show that Plato is himself a deeply traditional writer, one who needs to be read in the same way that we read the poets, whose embeddedness in their traditions we do not question or balk at. As a traditional writer Plato is like Diotima: he sees tradition as something that must be kept alive by questioning and that must be forced to live up to the demands of ever-new situations and ever-new inhabitants. New foundations, new beginnings, do not flourish through the complete rejection of the old ways. Instead, they require the questioning, critical, and caring attitude toward the received that we find in Socrates. Plato shows us how living within the tradition makes the new world possible.

PLATO AND TRADITION

PART I

Eros and Tradition

CHAPTER 1

Alcibiades I and Pederasty

The Neoplatonic philosophers believed that the study of Plato should begin
with the *Alcibiades* I. I similarly will begin my study of Plato's literary and
philosophical craft with this dialogue. The authenticity of *Alcibiades* I has
sometimes been doubted, though I do not believe that a compelling case has
been made for rejecting Plato's authorship.[1] Whether it was in fact written
by Plato or not, the dialogue does powerfully and clearly demonstrate and
introduce the creative approach to the traditional institutions of Athens that
I will argue is characteristic of the Platonic dialogues.

I will begin by recapitulating the basic conversation the dialogue presents
between Alcibiades and Socrates. I will then look at the particular ways in
which the theme of learning is explicitly and implicitly raised in this conversation to show the significance of tradition. Next I will look at Socrates's
discussion of his love for Alcibiades to show how what Socrates and, through
him, Plato, present through this understanding of eros is both a continuation
and a radical transformation of the Athenian institution of pederasty. It is
this transformative enactment of tradition that we will see, through the ensu-
ing chapters, to be characteristic of the Platonic writings.

The Conversation of *Alcibiades* I

As is so often the case in Platonic dialogues, Socrates's conversation with
the young Alcibiades in *Alcibiades* I is a conversation about competence: in
this instance about Alcibiades's competence to give advice at a meeting of
the Athenian assembly (105a–b, 106c) and about Socrates's competence to
help Alcibiades achieve all of his ambitions (105d–e). This second point,
Socrates's competence to help Alcibiades, is what moves the conversation,
when Alcibiades asks Socrates how it is that *Socrates* can help him more than
any other and Socrates offers to show (*endeixasthai*) Alcibiades that he can
(106a–b). Socrates's demonstration will take the form of a series of questions
for Alcibiades to answer (106b). The first line of questioning concerns what

precisely it is about which Alcibiades will be able to advise the Athenians and why precisely Alcibiades will be the one who is able to give this advice (106c and following). The subject of Alcibiades's advice and the reason that he will be in a position to give advice, it seems, rest on the fact that he will be advising about things that he knows better than the Athenians do (106d). More precisely, Alcibiades will be giving advice to the Athenians about their own affairs (*peri tōn hautōn pragmatōn*) (107c), more specifically, about war and peace or something else of that kind (107d). More precisely still, it emerges, Alcibiades will be giving advice about waging war or not, against whom to wage war and against whom not, and when to wage war and when not, in terms of the wars being just (109c).

Having clarified, through questioning, what Alcibiades thinks he will be giving advice to the Athenians about, Socrates turns to the questioning of Alcibiades's competence to give advice about justice. The two agreed at the beginning of Socrates's demonstration that Alcibiades would give advice about matters he knows better than the Athenians. They agreed, further, that there are two ways to come to know something: to learn it from others (*par' allōn emathes*) or to discover it by oneself (*autos exēures*) (106d). Socrates, then, expresses some surprise at 109d, when Alcibiades agrees that he will be giving advice about the justice of war, asking if Alcibiades has had some teacher of the more just and the more unjust of whom Socrates was unaware. Alcibiades asks in return whether he could not have come to know what is just and what is unjust in some other way (109e), to which Socrates replies that he could have if he had discovered it himself (109e), the second way of coming to know agreed on at 106d, which Socrates then sets out to show cannot have been the case. This demonstration rests on another point settled at 106d, that learning and discovering both depend on the learner's being willing (*ethelein*) to learn because he sees that he does not understand something. So, at 109e and following, Socrates shows Alcibiades that he has always believed himself to know what is just and unjust, even as a child (109e–110c). Alcibiades insists, at 110c, that he thought that he understood the just and unjust things as a child and that he *did* understand them (110c5), but he does acknowledge that perhaps he had not discovered the just and the unjust things on his own, but had, instead, learned them, just as other people do (*hōsper kai hoi alloi*) (110d).

Socrates then notes that the conversation has returned to the same point, by turning to the matter of learning from someone: "Who, then," Socrates asks, "is that someone? (*para tou;*)" (110d9). Socrates's question asks for a singular someone (*tou*) who can be declared or pointed out: "declare him to me, too (*phraze k'amoi*)," he says. Alcibiades's answer, however, is that his teachers were plural and vague: he learned *para tōn pollōn*, "from the many" (110e). Socrates is immediately dismissive of Alcibiades's answer, telling him that he has not taken refuge with serious teachers (*spoudaious didaskalous*) in referring his knowledge to the many (110e1–2), since the many are not even good teachers of the board game *petteia* (110e). Nonetheless, Alcibiades insists that the many can in fact teach many other things more serious than *petteia*. Specifically, Alcibiades says (111a1–4), "I myself learned to speak Greek (*hellēnizein*) from them, and I wouldn't be able to tell my teacher, but I refer it to the same people who you say are not serious teachers." Socrates agrees that the many would be good teachers of Greek because they know Greek and so can teach it (knowing something being the first condition of teaching it) (111a–b). What Socrates agrees that the many know, in knowing how to speak Greek, is what the names of things are: the many agree about what things are sticks, stones (111b–c), people, and horses (111d). This putting of the shared names to things in the world, Socrates says, is what he takes Alcibiades to mean when he speaks of understanding how to speak Greek (*hellēnizein epistasthai*) (111c3); Alcibiades assents to this assertion. What the many are *not* able to do, Socrates notes, is to make distinguishing judgments, such as recognizing and agreeing on a good racehorse or recognizing and agreeing on a healthy human being (111d–e) or recognizing and agreeing on just and unjust people and deeds (111e–112a). The ability to make distinguishing judgments with which others capable of making the same kind of distinguishing judgments will agree is here the hallmark of knowledge and the ability to teach (111b–c). So the many, Alcibiades agrees, do not know what just and unjust things are because they cannot agree amongst themselves what just and unjust things are, and so they cannot have taught Alcibiades what just and unjust things are (112d). Thus the question remains, how can Alcibiades know just and unjust things when he never learned them from another or discovered them himself (112d)?

Learning Language

I have provided this lengthy account of the opening pages of Socrates's demonstration of his importance to Alcibiades because, for my purposes here, the crux of this discussion emerges only *through* the conversation: it is not capable of being pointed to directly (much like Alcibiades's teacher of just and unjust things). Socrates maintains throughout this conversation that there are two ways and two ways only to come to know something, discovering it oneself and learning it from another. When Socrates provides examples of learning something from another, he illustrates learning from another as a matter of explicit *instruction,* a passing of knowledge from an expert to a nonexpert. (Alcibiades learned spelling, lyre-playing, and the like from teachers as he was growing up [106e]; but, he asks, who taught Alcibiades about just and unjust things? [106d]). When Alcibiades proposes another kind of learning from another, namely, learning from the many, and thus is unable to name a teacher, Socrates agrees that that is a kind of coming to know, but does not want to pursue it, turning the discussion instead back to the realm of knowledge as expertise. Alcibiades has, though, pointed to a real way of learning in this appeal to "the many" as his teacher of Greek: he has pointed to an *environmental* learning that impresses itself on all people without their necessarily being aware of it. Alcibiades points here to the same kind of learning that informs the jury at Socrates's trial in the *Apology.*

The jury at Socrates's trial has grown up with an image of Socrates as sophist and investigator of nature. Socrates cannot name the first accusers who have developed this "Socrates," and he cannot defend himself against them because growing to adulthood in Athens in the last decades of the fifth century involves "learning" that "Socrates" is a wise man who makes the worse argument the stronger and who investigates the things in the sky and the things under the earth.[2] Though this "knowledge" could be dismissed as gossip or trivial hearsay, Socrates himself here recognizes that such telling and retelling of stories within a group is in fact a process through which a shared, cultural perception is formed: it is not so much the explicit passing on of a content as it is the implicit establishing of a form of perception.[3] Alcibiades's learning Greek from the many and the jury's learning Socrates from the many are both examples of the same kind of environmental hearsay knowledge.[4]

I want to pursue more fully the significance of the idea that Alcibiades learned to speak Greek from the many. What is the nature of this kind of learning? What role does this kind of learning play in *Alcibiades* I as a whole? What can we learn from the account of this kind of learning in *Alcibiades* I about reading Platonic dialogues in general? When Alcibiades says that one of the serious things that he learned from the many was how to speak Greek, he says, "Just as I myself learned to speak Greek from them, and I wouldn't be able to tell who my teacher was [*kai ouk an echoimi eipein emautou didaskalon*—which can also be rendered 'I wouldn't be able to say there was a teacher of me'], but I refer it to the same people who you say are not serious teachers" (111a1–4). I will begin by considering how it is that Alcibiades can truly and accurately say that he learned Greek from the many.

Note first that Alcibiades does not refer here to any explicitly instructional relationship: he cannot say that there was a teacher for him in this regard. He does not see the learning of the Greek language, then, as the same learning that he experienced when he was taught spelling, lyre-playing, and wrestling by paid expert tutors.[5] Note also that Alcibiades does not credit his family with having taught him Greek. His learning of Greek, then, is not, to Alcibiades, a part of the world of the household: his learning of Greek is part of the world of the many, which is the shared world of the polis. Alcibiades's knowledge of Greek can be seen to have come about as a result of his immersion in an arena of fully developed linguistic competence and through some kind of participation in a community of Greek-speakers. His Greek is not the Greek of the women's quarters (the place for small children within the household), limited in its perspective to the language appropriate to the child.[6] Alcibiades attributes his Greek to the world of men in public. His knowledge of the language has come about through immersion in this world, interaction with men in that world, and initiation into full adult male status (marked in the dialogue by his being about to address the assembly for the first time, something possible only for a full adult male citizen in Classical Athens).

Language learned in this way is very much "hearsay": the child listens and repeats what he has heard, and as we grow up we adopt the language practices we encounter around us. We see such hearing and repeating on Alcibiades's part when, for example, he says that just things are not the same as advantageous things (113d), or when he characterizes his participation in politics as a competition against his fellow citizens (*antagōnizesthai . . . hōs ep' athlētas*). In these speeches, Alcibiades expresses typical elite Athenian views about action in general and politics in particular. Elite Athenian men conceive themselves always as in competition with other elite Athenian men for prestige and status, and their ability to compete successfully depends in part on a clear recognition of what will and will not tend to their advantage. So, in taking up the speech of men, Alcibiades has also taken up the *stances* of men. The world in which language is shared is the world in which understanding, belief, and value are shared. Along with how to *speak* Greek Alcibiades learned how to *be* Greek.[7]

Alcibiades, in learning Greek from the many, has learned the Greek that all Athenians share in the places that all Athenians share while engaged in the activities that all Athenians share. The shared spaces include the agora, the gymnasium, the theaters, the streets, and the acropolis. The shared activities include buying and selling, playing games, wrestling and exercising, religious festivals, attending the law courts, attending the assembly, and just hanging around. It is these activities of inhabiting these places that Alcibiades learned in learning Greek.

In learning how to speak Greek from the many, then, Alcibiades has learned more than how to use the shared names for things in the world. He can do more than understand what object someone intends when he says "stone" or "stick." Alcibiades has learned that, as "man" and "Athenian," he needs to do certain things (engage competitively in politics, for example) that are not contained simply in some lexical account of what "man" or "Athenian" means. Immanent in these words are ideas, values, and patterns of action the understanding of which is shared by other Athenians and other Greeks. This understanding is itself rooted in the shared life of people within the polis, which is something that stretches back in time over centuries. What Alcibiades has learned is a *tradition*. As a speaker of Greek, Alcibiades participates in and practices "traditional referentiality" in that his use of language is a way of carrying on a culturally shared perspective, rather than a one-to-one mapping of words to things.[8]

Alcibiades's claim that he learned to speak Greek from the many, then, draws our attention to some important aspects of language. Language is not only a giving of names that everyone recognizes and agrees on to objects in the world. It is also a sharing and a means of sharing of values, beliefs, and commitments that we do not learn simply by being instructed in them by experts or tutors. We learn them and take them up, often unbeknownst to ourselves, by participating in all of the activities in which we live through speaking, through living a life within a community.

Socrates's Knowledge

Within the dialogue, Socrates himself participates in the knowledge of hearsay. We see this participation most clearly in his accounts of the lives of the Great King of Persia and of the Spartan kings at 121a–123e. In these pages, Socrates trots out for Alcibiades a series of pieces of "knowledge" about the education of the Great King (121b–122b) and the virtues and wealth of the Spartan kings (122c–123a) that are fairly typical of the kinds of things that Athenians of the Classical period "know" and say about Persians and Spartans: The royal household of Persia is the focus of all of the economic activity of the Persian Empire (121c–d, 123b–c); The royal household of Persia is staffed by eunuchs (121d); All Persians are subject to serve the royal household (121e–122b); All Persians spend enormous amounts of their wealth on luxuries and on the display of their wealth, especially the Great King (122c, 123b–c). Socrates shares in the typical Greek portrayal of the Persians as luxurious, enslaved to the royal household, and marked by the practice of castrating men to serve in the women's quarters of the royal household.[9]

In the same way, Socrates's account of the Spartan kings provides a typical Athenian account of Sparta. The Spartan ephors have the role of watching over the households of their kings (121b–c). The Spartan elite are paragons of virtue (122c). The personal wealth of the Spartans, especially of the kings, surpasses that of all other Greeks (122d–e). Again Socrates offers Alcibiades an account of Spartans that is typical of how Athenians, particularly Athenian admirers of the Spartan way of life, describe Spartans.[10]

My point here is that Socrates presents Alcibiades with an authoritative account of the Persians and the Spartans that does not at any point *justify* its own authority. Socrates does not tell Alcibiades how he knows these things, with the exception of his reference to the Persian land called "the queen's girdle" at 123b–c, which he says he heard about from a man worthy of trust (*andros axiopistou*) (123b3–4).[11] Socrates does not offer himself as an eyewitness to any of the things he mentions; he does not tell Alcibiades that he has heard these things from others who have seen them; and he does not claim to have read them in books. Socrates tells Alcibiades about the resources of the Great King and of the Spartan kings to impress upon Alcibiades his own lack of resources in the face of these men and their peoples (121b, 123c–124b). Alcibiades must come to see, as Socrates says, that the only area in which he can possibly compete with these men on an equal footing is in taking care and in skill (*epimeleiai . . . kai technēi*) (124b2–3), which is what Socrates can help him in attaining. Consequently, it is essential to the success of Socrates's persuasion of Alcibiades that Alcibiades feel the force of this comparison between himself and his rivals. Alcibiades has to accept Socrates's account of the Great King and the Spartan kings as true.

The dialogue gives every evidence of Alcibiades's accepting this account as true, since Alcibiades does in fact yield to the force of Socrates's illustration and say to him, "you very much seem like someone who has said true things (*eoikas alēthē eirēkoti*)" (124b8–9). Alcibiades wants to know how he is to take care for himself, in light of what Socrates has said (*tina oun chrē tēn epimeleian . . . poieisthai*) (124b7–8). For Alcibiades to accept Socrates's point here, he has to have found the data Socrates uses to be uncontroversial and plausible. Certainly elsewhere in this dialogue Alcibiades is prepared to disagree with Socrates and to challenge him, even after he has been convinced of the necessity of his learning how to take care for himself.[12] In this passage, Socrates relies on Alcibiades's accepting his data, on his sharing some knowledge and understanding of the Spartans and Persians with him. Socrates relies on their sharing a body of knowledge that has come to them by virtue of the fact that they are Athenian men and so they know the kinds of things that Athenians know—they share a culture just as they share a language.

I want to draw attention here, then, to the fact that Socrates, like Alcibiades, has grown up in and been informed by a world that has provided him with a body of knowledge, a set of beliefs, and an understanding of the way things are. In his conversation, Socrates rightly assumes that he and Alcibiades share all of these things. Socrates's own relationship to the knowledge, attitudes, and expectations typical of Athenians is, of course, not always the same as that of most of his interlocutors. Repeatedly throughout the Platonic corpus, we see Socrates's critical stance toward this Athenian culturation. *Alcibiades* I provides no exception to this pattern. Indeed, one of the things that we see happening in this dialogue is Socrates's *use* of and *transformation* or *refiguring* of aspects of Athenian culture in his persuasion of Alcibiades. Most prominent is his reworking of the conventions of Athenian pederasty as he persuades Alcibiades to accept his love.

Socratic Love

In his comparison of Alcibiades's resources to those of the Great King and the Spartan kings, Socrates first describes the birth and education of the Great King (121b–122a). He then describes Alcibiades's education: Pericles appointed as Alcibiades's tutor (*paidagōgos*) a slave who was useless because of his old age (*achreiotaton hupo gērōs*), Zopyras the Thracian (122a8–b2). In Alcibiades's case no care was given to his education. Indeed, Socrates says, Alcibiades's birth, rearing, and education (*genos, trophē,* and *paideia*), just like those of any Athenian, were not a care to (*melei*) anyone, unless someone happened to love Alcibiades, to be his *erastēs* (122b). Here, Socrates explicitly links care and education to the context of Classical Athenian pederasty, in which an older man, the *erastēs,* initiates an adolescent beloved, the *erōmenos,* into social and political life in exchange for sexual favor.[13] In this case, of course, the lover who cares about Alcibiades's education is Socrates. The dialogue, purporting to be Socrates's first conversation with Alcibiades, opens with Socrates declaring himself to be the young man's lover. At 103a1–4, Socrates distinguishes himself from Alcibiades's other lovers by saying that he was the first to become Alcibiades's lover, and, now that all of the other lovers have left, he is the only one who has not changed from his love.

Socrates introduces himself to Alcibiades by insisting that, although he is like many other Athenian men in loving Alcibiades, he is not a typical lover. Most obviously, he does not love Alcibiades according to the traditional norms of Athenian pederasty, which dictate that the beloved be an adolescent citizen and the lover an adult citizen man. The boy becomes an appropriate object of desire when he reaches puberty; he ceases to be desirable when he achieves adult status at eighteen years of age. So, now that Alcibiades is an adult and his beauty, in Athenian pederastic terms, is beginning to fade,

his lovers have left him (103a, 131c, 131e–132a). Socrates, however, has remained Alcibiades's lover because, he says—and this is the deeper way in
which Socrates's love is not typical—he alone of Alcibiades's lovers loved
Alcibiades: loved his soul, not his body (131e–132a). Socrates, then, participates in a standard Athenian cultural practice, loving a beautiful boy, but
participates in a transformed way: he loves a boy who is beautiful in his soul,
and, as long as the soul remains beautiful, will continue to love him (132a).

As I noted above, Socrates links being Alcibiades's lover with having care
for his birth, rearing, and education (at 122b). In this concern, Socrates is
also typical of an Athenian lover. One of the primary social functions of a
pederastic relationship was, essentially, the initiation of the boy-beloved into
aspects of adult male social life, especially the forming of ties that would
be useful for political activity. In this sense, then, all lovers are concerned
with the rearing and education of their beloveds. Again, Socrates sets himself
apart from the traditional lover through the precise nature of the education
that he wants to give Alcibiades. While he claims that, like any lover, he will
be able to help Alcibiades to achieve political success (105e, 124b), he rejects
the standard view of achieving political success as dominating the assembly
(105a–c, 134c) and replaces it with his own: political success rests in giving
excellence to the citizens (134b–c). If Alcibiades is to have this kind of political success, he must possess excellence himself; this is the area in which
Socrates can help him (134c–135e). Again, then, Socrates promises to behave
toward Alcibiades in terms familiar to him as part of the received function
of pederastic relationships in Athens, and, again, Socrates marks himself as
enacting these terms in a transformed way. The structure of the relationship
that he proposes to Alcibiades is a traditional structure (adult lover and boy
beloved), the function of the relationship likewise is a traditional function
(preparation of the boy beloved for entry into political life); untraditional are
the terms of Socrates's love for Alcibiades (love of the beautiful adult soul
rather than the beautiful adolescent body) and the nature of the preparation
(assisting toward excellence rather than the forging of social ties).

The New Pederasty

Athenian pederasty had its own conventions, which, doubtless, were followed
more and less rigorously by living Athenians. It is these conventions that
Plato (or the author of *Alcibiades* I) works with in *Alcibiades* I. At the heart of
these conventions lies the agonism in which so many aspects of male life in
Classical Athens were rooted.[14] The lover wants his beloved; in particular he
wants to have anal intercourse with him, an expression of his dominance. The

beloved, on the other hand, wants a lover, but does not want to receive anal intercourse from his lover. To be known to have accepted anal penetration is to be shamed, to be regarded as not manly. Consequently, the lover must overcome the beloved's resistance, compelling the boy somehow to yield to him. The pederastic relationship, then, is to a large extent combative, and the relation of lover and beloved one of dominance and submission.[15]

Alcibiades I presents the process by which Socrates compels his beloved Alcibiades to yield to him. The submission that Socrates seeks from Alcibiades is not sexual submission, but the submission of his will, his spirit, and his understanding. Their conversation begins with Socrates noting just how high-spirited and proud Alcibiades is: many proud (*megalophrōn*) men have loved Alcibiades, but each of them, surpassed in pride (*huperblētheis tōi phronēmati*) by Alcibiades, has fled because Alcibiades is excessively proud (*huperphronein*) (103b2–104a1). Alcibiades's excessive pride rests, Socrates says, in his belief that he has no need of anyone for anything (104a1–2). Although it is a difficult thing for a lover to approach a man who is not bested by lovers (*ouch hēttona erastōn*), Socrates has come to speak to Alcibiades (104e4–6). What Socrates hopes Alcibiades will be convinced of is that he does in fact have need of Socrates because, Socrates claims, Alcibiades will not be able to achieve his great ambitions for power and glory without Socrates (105c–d).

Alcibiades, as Socrates presents it, has driven away all of the men who wanted to be accepted as his lover because Alcibiades does not think that he needs a lover to do what lovers typically do in Athens: help him in his political career. Alcibiades believes that he already possesses in himself all the resources necessary to have success: beauty, family connections (particularly his relationship with Pericles), and wealth (104a–c). He also believes that he himself has the talent and charisma to achieve dominance over the Athenian assembly (105a–b). Alcibiades, Socrates claims, seems to think himself unique among Athenians in that he will be able to become politically dominant in Athens, and consequently in Greece and Europe (105b–c), without behaving like other Athenian politicians, without beginning an adult political career drawing on the social resources of an older and more influential lover. To enter into a pederastic relationship could be desirable to Alcibiades only if such a relationship could help his political career; if he does not need that help, he has no need of a lover.

So what Socrates must compel Alcibiades to see is that he *needs* to accept Socrates as his lover. To make his case, Socrates must get Alcibiades to clarify his understanding of what precisely it is that he desires and of how it is that this desire can be fulfilled; then he must come to see the unique ability of Socrates to participate in, assist in, that achieving. Alcibiades, to accept

Socrates as his lover, must come to see that he is *not* self-sufficient and that, just as he is one of a kind among young aspiring politicians, so Socrates is one of a kind among mature aspiring lovers. It is through their uniqueness that Socrates and Alcibiades are suited to each other.

The dialogue presents to us the path by which Socrates compels Alcibiades to submit to him, to be bested by a lover. Socrates does not follow the conventional Athenian practices of bringing gifts, begging for sex, or using physical violence;[16] his compulsion takes the form of typical Socratic question and answer. Through his conversation, Socrates forces Alcibiades to yield to him his sense of his own ability to understand and think, his sense of himself as self-sufficient. As we have seen, when Alcibiades is not willing simply to adhere to the terms of Socrates's questions, Socrates dismisses Alcibiades's resistance, his attempts to come to grips with the substance of their conversation and not merely its forms. What I want to notice here is that, true as this conclusion about Alcibiades's self-understanding may be, Socrates brings us to this conclusion through a kind of unfair conversational compulsion. By insisting so firmly on our learning either through our own discovery or through instruction by others, and by mocking Alcibiades's suggestion that the many could teach anything important, Socrates dismisses a genuine attempt at understanding, a valuable contribution to a discussion of how it is that we learn, when Alcibiades puts it forward.

When Alcibiades tells Socrates that he knows and understands the just and unjust things, Socrates gets Alcibiades to agree that one comes to know something either by discovering it oneself or by being instructed in it. Since Alcibiades did not discover the just and unjust things on his own and received no instruction in them, he cannot know and understand them. Trying to explain how it is that he can correctly say that he knows the just and the unjust things Alcibiades offers a third kind of learning, learning from the many, as he learned to speak Greek from the many. As I have argued, Alcibiades appeals here to the way in which people learn from their environment, how they become participant members in their culture, fluent in its language and its values. Socrates does not allow that there is such learning and dismisses the many as teachers of anything by getting Alcibiades to agree that learning how to speak Greek involves only the learning of the names of things, which is a trivial knowledge, unlike the knowledge of the just and the unjust things. The discussion of Alcibiades's knowledge of just and unjust things ends at 116e with Alcibiades confessing to Socrates that he has no idea what he is saying and that his sense of what they are talking about is constantly changing. He is confused (*planasthai*) (117a10), which, Socrates tells him, is an indication that he does not know the just and unjust things

(117a). Socrates goes on to lead Alcibiades to agree that when people do not know things, they need to get someone who does know these things to take charge, as people hand over control to the helmsman of a ship (117a–d). Alcibiades's vision of himself as self-sufficient in this conversation is thus shown to be false: he does not know the just and unjust things (although he thought he did), and so he needs someone who does know them to instruct him in them and make decisions about them on his behalf.

While the ultimate conclusions they reach about Alcibiades's lack of self-sufficiency may well be true, Socrates's method involves a bit of cheating. First, as I have said, Socrates bypasses a real insight that could have been gleaned from Alcibiades's answers. Second, despite his insistence at 112d–113b that Alcibiades is the one who is directing their conversation through his answers to Socrates's questions, Socrates is the one who makes the decisions and who determines where the conversation will lead so that he can achieve his goal of convincing Alcibiades that he needs Socrates, which is, of course, the express purpose of this entire conversation.

Another such episode of resistance, dismissal, and submission occurs at 127b–d, in the discussion of how *philia* and same-mindedness (*homonoia*) arise in a city. Socrates and Alcibiades have agreed that people avoid making mistakes when each sticks to his own thing, the thing about which he knows. How, Socrates asks, can same-mindedness arise for people when they do not understand the same things (126e)? Alcibiades admits that it cannot (127a). And so, Socrates says, since *philia* is the same as same-mindedness (126c), there can be no *philia* between people who do not have same-mindedness (127a). Therefore cities in which all the people do their own things cannot be well-run cities because there is no *philia* and no same-mindedness among citizens (127b). At this point, Alcibiades says that it seems to him that it is precisely in each doing his own thing that *philia* is in fact possible in cities (127b). Socrates reminds Alcibiades that, according to everything they have agreed on so far, what Alcibiades now says cannot be the case, cannot make sense (127c). Alcibiades agrees and admits that he does not know what he is saying and that, further, he has probably not known what he is talking about for a long time without even knowing it (127d). He wonders what someone who comes to understand this fact about himself should do; Socrates tells him that he should answer the questions (127e).

Again we see Socrates sticking to the terms of the conversation and insisting that Alcibiades pursue the thread of the conversation by remaining faithful to what has been agreed on. Alcibiades's point that *philia* does in fact arise in cities when people do their own things cannot be sensible here if *philia* is the same as same-mindedness, a point to which Alcibiades himself has agreed. Nonetheless, to say that *philia* arises when people do their own things is a substantial claim to make, one deserving of consideration. This claim is not capable of being pursued here because Socrates insists on there being a simple synonymy of *philia* and same-mindedness. When Alcibiades says that cities are well-run when there is *philia* present among the people, Socrates asks him, do you mean by *philia* "*homonoia*" (same-mindedness) or "*dichonoia*" (divided-mindedness) (126c)? Alcibiades means *homonoia*. Socrates does not *ask* Alcibiades what he means when he says *philia*; he offers him a choice of two things he could mean, one of which Alcibiades could not possibly mean. He offers this choice as a choice of simple identity; he does not say, "and by *philia*, among other things do you mean *homonoia* or *dichonoia*?" When Alcibiades makes the obvious choice, *homonoia*, he is then stuck with an interchangeable synonym. In this way, his claim that *philia* comes to be when people do their own things really does not make sense.

But it is *only* in this way that this claim does not make sense. Alcibiades's confusion at 127e arises not merely from a recognition that he does not know what he is talking about (the thing that Socrates has to get him to see) but surely also from a sense that he *does* know what he is talking about, that *philia* does come about in cities when people do their own thing and that part of the problem has to be that he does not know how to say what he knows and understands in this conversation with this Socrates. Socrates compels Alcibiades's submission, his request for help (what should someone who knows that he is confused do?), through a conversational *method* and through a strict adherence to that method. It is the moments at which Alcibiades resists that method, offering alternatives to the syllogistic path that Socrates wants him to follow, that afford Socrates the best occasions for forcing Alcibiades's submission. This passage is the last time that Alcibiades offers any resistance to Socrates; from here Socrates leads Alcibiades through a series of questions and assents in which Alcibiades follows Socrates's lead and accepts all of the conclusions at which they arrive.[17]

Socrates, then, offers a transformation of the traditional Athenian institution of pederasty, maintaining the basic form, but bringing to it new terms that come from defining the person in terms of soul—a self-conscious inside—rather than in terms of body—an outside that figures in the consciousness of others. This transformed sense of love, however, brings with it new possibilities for force, and Socrates equally demonstrates through his behavior a new argumentative compulsion—sophistry—to replace the physical compulsion that marked the old pederasty. Though we should appreciate the advance of introducing the theme of "love of soul," we should not be blind to the possibilities for new forms of abuse that this transformation brings with it.

The New Eros as a Challenge to Athenian Culture

There are other aspects of Socrates's offer to assist Alcibiades toward excellence that rework typical Athenian practice and custom. Socrates tells Alcibiades that his birth, rearing, and education are a concern to no one except a lover, citing Pericles's lack of care in choosing a *paidagōgos* for Alcibiades. Birth, rearing, and education of a boy in Classical Athens were primarily the responsibility of the family, except for the acknowledging of an infant as a citizen birth by the father's phratry (kin-descent group) and the boy's participation in various city-based religious activities, such as performing in a boys' chorus.[18] Socrates's account of the education of the Great King at 121d–122b also marks the household as the place in which education of the young takes place. The infant king is attended by eunuchs in the king's service (121d). When the king is a child, he is handed over to instructors of riding and learns how to hunt (121e). As an adolescent, he receives instruction in virtue from the royal tutors (*basileious paidagōgous*) (121e–122b). The royal household oversees the birth, rearing, and education of its boys.

As Socrates tells it, the household of the Great King is exemplary for the care it gives to the bringing up of its boys. Pericles's household, on the other hand, has utterly failed to live up to its responsibility to educate Alcibiades, as all other Athenian households have failed their own boys. In Alcibiades's case, at least, Socrates offers himself, as Alcibiades's lover, as the one who will take care for Alcibiades's bringing up: he offers to replace the household with the lover. Alcibiades has not been failed just by his guardian, Pericles, though. The dialogue reminds us of Alcibiades's orphan status at 104b, when Socrates remarks that Alcibiades's father made Pericles Alcibiades's guardian.[19] Alcibiades was the ward of Pericles because Alcibiades's father, Cleinias, died at the battle of Coroneia in 447 B.C.E. In democratic Athens, the city itself took responsibility for the education of war orphans and for assisting boys in beginning their adult citizen life, chiefly by providing boys with a hoplite panoply when they came of age.[20] Democratic Athens, then, did the family's work when the family could not look after its own. She replaced the household with the polis.

Socrates's offer to educate Alcibiades reworks *two* Athenian cultural practices, pederasty and democratic ideology. Socrates, in offering to take care for Alcibiades's upbringing, is offering to take up the responsibilities of the household and of the city. In his version of the pederastic relationship, both family and city are replaced by the lover. Plato here evokes two received aspects of Athenian culture and tradition that serve as the ground for Socrates's offer to Alcibiades (Socrates's behavior is recognizable and comprehensible as typically pederastic) and that are transfigured by the precise terms in which Socrates wants his relationship with Alcibiades to work (as educational).[21] This reworking at least marks the radical nature of what Socrates proposes to Alcibiades: the creation of an erotic arena of commitment for the pursuit of excellence that is neither the household nor the polis, and which will serve to supplant them.[22]

The *Symposium* and Sappho

In this chapter, I shall be asking Sappho, through a discussion of some of her fragments, and Plato, through a discussion of Diotima's account of eros in the *Symposium,* "What is love?" I shall begin by exploring how love manifests itself in Sappho's poems; from an analysis of fragments 5, 94, and 55, I will argue that Sappho provides us with a notion of love as *care*.[1] In particular, Sappho shows us that love is embedded in relationships of reciprocity of action and feeling that result in sharing responsibilities to and understandings of the world. Turning next to *Symposium* 201d–212c, I shall argue that Diotima's account of eros is by and large the same as Sappho's account of the mutual responsibilities of care. Diotima tells the story of the education of eros, taking eros from simple desire for a lovely body to desire for understanding of the beautiful itself. This educated—philosophical—eros, which continues to act through care, reveals itself as the foundation of the human capacity to have a tradition, to have great poetry, to develop technology, to live in groups with laws and constitutions. This eros that Diotima develops is a far cry from the overwhelming, driving, maddening thing that the Greeks generally take eros to be.[2] Consequently, in the third section of this chapter I shall address the question of what is in fact *erotic* about Diotima's eros. Again I shall look first to Sappho to provide an account of compulsive eros that drives us and makes us forgetful of ourselves and our ties of care to the rest of the world. When we look back to Diotima in light of Sappho, we shall see that her eros, too, is compulsive; it is a part of our nature (*phusis*) to feel desire that we cannot control or avoid and that makes us forget who we are. For both Sappho and Diotima, eros has the capacity to keep us absorbed in the "now" and is a wild thing, able to undermine the social world of law and tradition. It is in this very wildness, I shall argue in the final section, that we see eros's real capacity to keep tradition *alive*, flourishing and moving, rather than static. Eros's demand that things be meaningful *to me* and meaningful *now* gives rise to people's ability, as groups with traditions, to take up what they inherit and be open to questioning and transforming the "received."

Plato, then, in writing *Symposium,* erotically (carefully and wildly) takes up traditional notions of eros and care found in Sappho, questions them, makes new *logoi* about them, and makes explicit the possibilities inherent in them.

Care

In colloquial English, one would commonly say "I love that film," or "I love that book." In just such a sense, I can say that I "love" Sappho: I love to read Sappho. In fact, I believe this idiom is not simply arbitrary: the issues involved in reading, I believe, are very much of a piece with the issues of love "proper." Let us consider, briefly, this "love" of Sappho.

That I love to read Sappho means in part that I take pleasure from those lines. My love of Sappho is thus to some degree self-indulgent: I love her for the pleasure she can give to me. But my relationship to this object of my love—"Sappho"—is not simply instrumental, as would be my relationship to a shoe, a strawberry, or a hot shower. Unlike these possible objects of desire, "Sappho" is a body of text, an expressive, meaningful unity. This object does not simply bend to my will, but offers me, rather, an inherent meaning, and inherent value, of its own. To love Sappho, then, is like loving a responsive, embodied human being, like my old friend or my student or my brother or the one who inhabits my dreams.

That love—the love for a person—is a love about which Sappho herself has much to say. With any person whom I love, I turn to that person to learn from the beloved how she or he is to be loved: this is what it means for the object of love to be intrinsically meaningful, and not simply an instrument. The Sappho that is the object of my love is similarly intrinsically meaningful and, indeed, speaks precisely of the nature and demands of love. For that reason, then, it is fitting to turn to Sappho—to the text itself—and to ask, "How should I love you?" Accepting that our reading does, indeed, evince a kind of love, we can learn from Sappho herself a lesson that is simultaneously erotic and hermeneutic.[3] In learning about love, we shall learn, too, about the demands of reading.

The love of persons, which we are taking as our model for the love of an author or a body of text, is a broad love, encompassing the many sorts of loving, interpersonal relations that fill our lives. This broad sense of love I will call "care." Erotic love, about which Sappho famously speaks powerfully, seems to be only one part of this broader love. Consequently, I shall begin my analysis from a poem in which Sappho talks, not about an erotic beloved, but about one of those for whom she cares—one of those she calls her "*philoi*"—namely, her brother. We turn our attention first, then, to fragment 5, the poem in which Sappho prays to Aphrodite and the Nereids for her brother's safe homecoming. What I shall do here is simply work through the poem to draw from it notions that are relevant to our interests. I will ask, "Since Sappho loves her brother, about what sorts of things is she driven to be concerned?"

Let us consider first the term "*philos*." *Philos* most fundamentally means "what belongs to me," what is "my own." We sometimes find it used in the *Iliad* and *Odyssey* almost as a possessive adjective, as with *philos thumos*, "his own (dear) spirit."[4] When people are the objects in question, we find that the group Greek literature designates as the "*philoi*" contains primarily my family, my friends, and my close associates. The *philoi* are the people who matter most to me. Specifically, they are those with whom my relationship is characterized by *aidōs*, a complicated notion. At heart, *aidōs* means "concern for the other": concern both for that person's view of oneself and for that person's well-being. My *philoi*, then, are the people whose view of me and whose well-being are crucial to me and to whom my view of them and my well-being are key. They are those with whom I am in relationships of reciprocal care.

With this understanding of the "*philoi*" in mind, let us now turn to Sappho's fragment 5 to see what it can tell us about how to participate in a relationship of reciprocal care.

> Cypris and Nereids, grant that
> My brother arrive here (*tuide*) unharmed for me (*ablabēn moi*)
> And that as many things (*k'ossa*) as he wants in his heart to
>   come to be
> All (*panta*) be accomplished,   4
>
> And that as many things he made mistakes about before he
>   pay for all of them
> And be a joy to his own *philoi*
> And a source of pain to his enemies (*echthroi*), and may not
>   even one man
> Still be grief to us;   8
>
> And may he wish to make his sister
> Having a share of honor (*emmoron timas*), and grievous
>   source of pain . . .
> . . . . previously being pained[5]

Beginning with the first stanza, let us notice first that, in her prayer, Sappho links herself to her brother: in lines 1–2, Sappho asks that her brother arrive here unharmed for her. The Greek here is *ablabēn moi;* the dative pronoun is a straightforward dative of interest, "to me" or "for me." The placement of the pronoun, immediately after the adjective, suggests that the interest here lies specifically in the intact state of her brother when he arrives, but does not preclude the sense that the pronoun is the indirect object of the verb, "grant," giving us the sense "grant *to me* that. . . ." Sappho's prayer, then, is a prayer offered for herself *and* for her brother, marking the fact that, in Sappho's view, her interests and her brother's interests are unified.

This initial request for a safe arrival is in fact a request for a safe arrival home. Sappho addresses her prayer here to Aphrodite and the Nereids, who shared a sanctuary on the island Lesbos, Sappho's home.[6] The use of the adverb "here" (*tuide*) in line 2 indicates that Sappho herself is on Lesbos—perhaps we envision her at the sanctuary itself—requesting a safe return home for her brother. The invocation of the Nereids in particular suggests that Sappho's brother has left not merely Mytilene, the polis on Lesbos to which Sappho and her family belonged, but Lesbos itself, as the Nereids are sea divinities, most properly invoked for protection and favor on sea journeys. This evocation of journey by sea and homecoming at the end of a sea journey further opens up possibilities of allusion to the *Odyssey,* to which I shall return shortly.

As we move to the next two lines of the stanza, we find the request that her brother accomplish everything that his spirit wishes.[7] These lines are not specific concerning the nature of her brother's desires but instead stress the indefiniteness (and hence completeness) of Sappho's wish: "*as many things* as he wants . . . *all* be accomplished" (*k̄ossa . . . panta*). Her care for him, then, in the first stanza, manifests itself as a concern for his physical safety and well-being; for his presence with her, at home, where he belongs; and for his ability to fulfill his own desires.

To a certain extent, the wishes of the first stanza can be seen as the wishes of the household: what concerns Sappho is her brother's presence with her and his self-satisfaction. The second stanza, on the other hand, moves from the concerns of the household to the concerns of the social group in that it contains wishes that her brother participate appropriately in group reciprocity. This concern manifests itself first as a request that her brother pay back, pay for, or requite all of the mistakes he has made in the past, however many they are (line 5). Here Sappho's attention is directed, not specifically at her brother or herself, but at her brother's dealings with others: that he be able to pay for all of his past errors demands that he be in a state of not owing anything to anyone else, that he be free of obligation incurred by circumstance (not obligation in general).

Sappho next requests that her brother be a joy to his *philoi* and a source of pain to his enemies (his *echthroi*) (lines 6–7). Sappho presents here a fairly typical traditional elite Greek notion of justice as helping one's friends and harming one's enemies.[8] Her request, then, is that her brother be able to participate appropriately in conventional relationships of reciprocal benefit and harm, that he be able, in essence, to achieve not only what he himself wants for himself but also what his people in general expect of an elite man. Sappho moves beyond the simply conventional in the next request, that not even one man still be a pain *to us* (*ammi*) (lines 7–8). Here, as in lines 1–2, she links herself explicitly with her brother in her wish for freedom from pain caused by, one assumes, enemies. Sappho thus implicates herself in her brother's activities within the group. The first two stanzas of fragment 5, then, set up prayers for Sappho's brother's well-being and success in Sappho's eyes, in her brother's eyes, and in the eyes of the group.

The third stanza begins with another wish, that her brother want to make Sappho one who has a share of honor (*emmoron timas*) (line 10).[9] In this wish we see, first of all, the reciprocity that should exist among *philoi:* I desire from my *philoi* the same concern for my success that I feel for their success. Sappho here asks that her brother desire for her what she desires for him. What she desires for him, in the first two stanzas, is that he achieve all he desires and that he inhabit his proper arena, the social arena of elite Greek men, appropriately and successfully. She further indicates, in her use of the phrase *emmoron timas,* in what arena her brother should wish for her success: the arena of poetry. *Emmoron timas* appears also at *Odyssey* 8.480 immediately following Demodocus's singing of the story of Ares and Aphrodite. At this point, Alcinous, king of the Phaeacians and Odysseus's host at the feast at which Demodocus performs, directs an attendant to take a portion of meat to Demodocus because singers are entitled to be cherished and to be "*emmoroi timas*" because the Muse loves them. Sappho marks her own sphere of activity here; links herself to a traditional figure, Demodocus; and asks that her brother desire that she achieve the same kind of success as a singer that Demodocus, loved by the Muse, has achieved.[10] Just as, in lines 5–8, Sappho wishes that her brother achieve success in a traditional social role, so here, in lines 9–10, Sappho asks that her brother desire for her success in a traditional social role. She sets up a precise parallel in the reciprocity between herself and her brother.[11]

In fragment 5, then, Sappho draws upon some of the basic aspects of care, of *aidōs,* between *philoi.* Care involves concern for the well-being of the other, desire for the presence of the other, desire for the success of the other, and desire for the other to manifest these same desires toward oneself. All of these concerns are expressed in a prayer, a speech designed to try to achieve the goals stated in the prayer. We can take from the prayer form itself, finally, that another aspect of care is actually to do something to assist the cared-for other in the achieving of goals. At the heart of care for Sappho, at least in fragment 5, is reciprocity. She cares, and she wants care in return.

Sappho's insistence here on the desire for reciprocity at the heart of care directs us to a number of her other poems that also stress notions of requital in kind and mutual desires. I shall focus in what follows on fragment 94, which portrays a conversation between Sappho and her beloved as the beloved prepares to leave Sappho.[12]

> . . . .
> And honestly I want to have died;
> She weeping much left me behind
>
> and said this, too. . . .
> Alas, how we have suffered terrible things (*hōs deina peponthamen*).
> Sappho, truly I am leaving you unwillingly.   5
> And I replied (*ameiboman*) these things to her;
> Go rejoicing and remember
> me (*k'amethen memnais'*), for you know how we cared for you;
>
> But if not, rather I want
> to remind you (*omnaisai*)   10
> . . . . we used to suffer fair things too (*kai kala epaschomen*)
>
> for with many crowns of violets
> and of roses and of crocuses . . . [13]

Reciprocity appears in this fragment most basically in its form: it is a conversation. "She" speaks to Sappho, addressing her by name at line 5, and Sappho replies. The verb used to designate reply here is *ameiboman*, from *ameibō*, which has at its root the notion of exchange, particularly when used in the middle voice, as here. When this verb is used to describe speech, it is used consistently to designate speech made in answer to another speech.[14]

In the second stanza, the first speaker alludes to the fact of her having a relationship with Sappho that has a past; she says at line 4, "how we have suffered terrible things" (*hōs deina peponthamen*). She reminds Sappho of their shared experience, more particularly, of their shared experience, it seems, of pain. Sappho takes up this statement in her own speech, telling the first speaker at line 11, "we also used to suffer fair things (*kai kala epaschomen*)." She uses the same verb, in the imperfect now rather than the perfect, to remind the young woman of another aspect of their shared experience: good things, pleasure, satisfaction. Sappho enacts here another aspect of care for the other. The first speaker has made a claim of fact, we have suffered terrible things. That claim is put forward without complication or mitigation as a full accounting of the truth of the experiences Sappho and the other speaker share. In a careful way, Sappho here corrects the first claim, not by denying it, but by insisting on its not being a complete account. There were terrible things in the past, but there were fair things as well.[15] Care here appears as care not just for physical well-being or the achievement of desires, but as care for the other's thought or understanding. If I care for someone, I cannot allow that person's thinking to be inaccurate, incomplete, or limited when I have the resources to complete it.[16]

Sappho's correction at line 11 is connected explicitly with memory. She tells the first speaker at lines 7–8, "remember me (*k'amethen memnais'*)" and adds at lines 9–10, "rather I want to remind you (*omnaisai*)." The first speaker has invoked memory in her speech, but Sappho makes explicit and stresses the fact of memory in her reply. The first speaker has tried, through her statement about their shared past, to create memory for Sappho; Sappho has responded in kind by creating memory, a more complete memory, for the first speaker. It is important to recall here that, in Archaic Greek poetry, memory is not thought of merely as a part of thought, but is understood as the calling of the past into a real living present.[17] In the context of fragment 94, we see the importance of Sappho's insistence on complete memory in light of what it is that memory does. The past cannot be truly remembered if the recollection is selective or one-sided. Fragment 94, then, adds to our notion of care in Sappho the importance of memory in the calling into presence of the loved other, a variation of Sappho's desire for the actual presence of her loved brother in fragment 5. Care here is responsible for preserving memory.[18]

I turn finally to fragment 55, which discusses, not love, but memory and, in particular, Archaic Greek poetry's emblem of memory par excellence, poetry itself.

> And having died you will lie nor ever will there be memory
>   (*mnamosuna*)
> of you not even ever later; for you do not share in the roses
> from Pieria; but unseen (*aphanēs*) even in the house of Hades
> you will wander flitting about with the dim dead.

It is not clear who the addressee of these lines is, but it does seem fairly clear that Sappho does not like her. The addressee will not be remembered (there will be no *mnamosuna,* line 1) after she dies because she did not have a share in the Muses (the roses from Pieria at lines 2–3),[19] that is, because she does not have a share of poetry. There is, then, no possibility of the calling of this woman into lived presence through the performance of poetry. When she is dead, she is done. In this fragment, the living presence is dependent not on love, but on poetry alone. We note, then, the function that love and poetry share: the preservation or inciting of memory. Sappho draws our attention here to the situation of the dead when there is no memory of them: not only do those alive not recall them but they are also invisible (*aphanēs,* line 3) among the dead. This woman, dead, will flit among the dim shadows; Sappho evokes here the situation of the tribes of the nameless dead Odysseus sees in *Odyssey* 11. Odysseus travels to the land of the dead to consult the soul of Teiresias, famed in song. While he is in the land of the dead, Odysseus sees or engages in conversation with souls of those famed in song, like Achilleus or Tityus or the famous Boeotian women. The fact of their having had a share in the Muses, of their having had a poet like Demodocus or Sappho sing of them, ensures that, even dead, they are remembered by the living and recognized by the other famous dead. Epic *kleos* (glory preserved in song) and Sappho's *mnamosuna* both achieve the same thing, the possibility of the preservation of memory and the calling into living presence of individuals through song.[20] In its way, this poem tells us something similar to fragment 5: Sappho desires in fragment 5 to be *emmoron timas,* to achieve success as a poet. Here in fragment 55, she reminds us of one of the things that her success as a poet will get for her: memory, the possibility of being called into living presence.

Careful Reading

So, if I care for, if I love this dead poet, what should I do for her? I should try, as fragment 5 tells me, to help her accomplish what she desires. Sappho's desire, as we see in fragments 94 and 55, is to be remembered, to be brought into living presence. This remembrance is accomplished by reading her poems and by reading them, as fragment 94 tells us, as completely as possible. Such completeness requires reading her in her specificity and in her totality. But since Sappho is a poet who lived on the other side of the planet almost three thousand years ago, a proper reading must excavate that dead world and learn her social, historical, poetic, and mythological context. The full, loving reading of Sappho is not simply aesthetic, not simply about the pleasure one can take in her beauty; the reading of Sappho is a matter of responsible investigation. Such a reading does not leave the reader untouched: if it is true that "I love Sappho," this means that I endeavor to make myself as much as possible one who can have shared experiences with her, one who has, as in fragment 94, suffered the same things she has.[21] It is from that sharing alone that I can call her into living presence, much as Sappho calls for the living presence of Aphrodite in fragment 2.

> coming down
> here to me from Crete . . . to a holy temple
>   where your graceful grove
> of apple trees is, and altars perfumed
> with frankincense . . .   5
> . . .
> here indeed you, Cypris,
> taking in golden cups nectar
> delicately mixed with festivities   15
>   pour.

The calling of the god into presence demands that we share a world with the god. Sappho indicates to Aphrodite in lines 1 to 2 that she knows some of the things the god knows, some of the things the god does; she knows about her great temple on Crete. Sappho requests the god's presence on Lesbos in a temple and sacred grove that the people of the place have built and dedicated to the god. Sappho, the people of Mytilene, and Aphrodite have an established relationship of worship and shared knowledge. Sappho asks Aphrodite to be present for a special occasion, a time of festivities (l. 15), of the gathering of people in honor of the god. So Sappho and her people share a world with the god. It is the shared human event (festivities in honor of Aphrodite) that provides the reason for the request. The calling of the god into presence, then, according to this poem, is an experience to be shared with members of one's own group, an experience that must take place in the public space of the temple and of group festivity.[22]

The living presence, then, is one to be shared. More, the living presence is possible only through sharing. If I call someone to mind through reading her poetry, I am calling someone to mind through participation in a *communicative act,* an act that desires others to recognize it as communicative and to attend to its message (the poem). The communicative act that is a poem is not one that is directed in a private way simply to me or to you in particular. The poet fulfills her desire for memory in an intensely promiscuous way—the poem is for anyone who happens to read it.[23] But those of us who have come to know and love this poet and who have attended carefully to her expression of her desires know how to begin, at least, to respond to her communication. We share her with others. Ideally, we share her with the type of others that she has marked as those who will best fulfill what her spirit desires. We share her with our own *philoi* in our own temples and at our own festivities. We bring Sappho alive into the world that we share with one another.

From Sappho, then, we learn that loving someone well, caring for that person, involves first that we want reciprocity—we want that person to love and care for us as we love and care for her or him (this point is most apparent in fragment 5). To care for another, we must, as fragments 5 and 94 both indicate, be prepared to *act* out of our care; we offer a prayer (a speech designed to achieve something in the world, to act), or we intervene to help the beloved think or remember well. Our actions out of care should be informed by our regarding our interests and our beloved's interests as intertwined; my beloved's well-being and success are integral to *my* well-being and success. We regard the beloved as *philos*, as our own. We share a world with our *philoi*. The success that we want for the ones we love is of two kinds: the general success of safety and full integration in the world, domestic and social, and the more particular success of achieving the goals that he or she sets out to achieve, as we see in fragment 5. At the same time, we want the beloved for ourselves—we long for the presence of that loved one, as Sappho longs for her brother's presence and as the young woman of fragment 94 looks forward to longing for Sappho. In the absence of the beloved, we depend on memory to keep the beloved before us. This memory, as fragment 94 indicates, should be a careful memory, as complete a recollection as possible. Memory must be as full as possible because the *living* presence of the beloved depends on it. We see in fragment 55 the function of poetry as a purveyor of memory. We remember Sappho as the poet who produced these pieces; we have kept her memory alive through continuing to read, study, and love these poems. These poems, this Sappho, are most alive, most present, when we attempt to share a world with them by learning about them, by learning about Sappho, and by learning what the world out of which these lovable poems arose was like.

Diotima

In what follows, my goal is to show that a notion of love and care very much like what we see in Sappho's poems drives Diotima's account of eros in the conversation she has with Socrates at *Symposium* 201d to 212c. Here we see that eros, desiring immortality, begins as a desire for a relationship of reciprocal care and responsibility with another person. Again we see that eros urges us to act and to intervene on behalf of the beloved in order to ensure the beloved's well-being and success; this intervention initially takes the form of trying to educate the beloved and helping him to manifest excellence (*aretē*). Diotima also notes our desire for the living presence of the beloved, fulfilled through spending time with him or through memory. For Diotima, eros only *begins* as a desire for another person; educated eros, philosophical eros, learns to desire, not a beautiful person, but beautiful *logoi,* through which humans best achieve their desire for immortality. It is in eros for *logoi* that we see memory most fully at play in the way that Sappho articulates it: the beautiful *logoi* that we produce and cherish remain alive through their being kept alive and beloved by others over time. For Diotima, as for Sappho, love and memory form the foundation of tradition.

The first and most significant fact about eros that Diotima and Socrates establish in their conversation is that eros is a desire for that of which people feel themselves to be in need (*endeēs*) (204a). Most generally what people feel themselves to need is the good (205e); to desire the good is to see it as something for me, something *oikeion* (205a–206e). The content of this desire for the good is that I want it to be mine forever (*to to agathon hautōi einai aei*) (206a6 and following). To have the good as mine forever, I must engage in some activity (*praxei*) (206b), which Diotima explains is "giving birth in the beautiful both in body and in soul" (206b7–8); we desire to give birth because all of us are, as soon as we arrive at a certain maturity (*hēlikiai*), pregnant in body and soul (206c1–4). So eros, then, is not desire for the beautiful but desire for the generation (*tēs gennēseōs*) and giving birth (*tokos*) in the beautiful (206e2–5).[24] What I desire is to reproduce, to put myself into the world in the production of something new that is mine.[25] This self-reproducing is *my* good, and it is an activity that is for me, it is *oikeion*. Since we desire the good to be ours forever (*aei*), Diotima says, what humans in fact desire is immortality (*athanasias*) (206e). This desire for immortality is present in all things that are by nature (*phusei*) (207c8); all mortal beings (wild animals, humans) try to be immortal (207b–d). For mortal beings, immortality as such is not possible; the only way in which we can be something like immortal is through bringing-into-being (*tēi genesei*), which leaves behind something new in place of the old (*anti tou palaiou*) (207d). It is by this device (*mēchanēi*) that the mortal has a share of immortality (208b).[26]

According to this discussion, all eros is, at its root, a desire to be immortal that is realized only through the production of something new; this production is *re*production, bringing-into-being a version of oneself out of oneself. This claim seems to fit well enough with sexual desire and the reproduction of the species (the immortal being) through the production of offspring, or the reproduction of two parents through their children. Diotima's point, though, is that *all* eros is desire for immortality. She offers as proof of this claim human *philotimia* (love of honor). This desire is seen when people want to become famous (*onomastoi*) and to store up immortal glory for all time (*kleos es ton aei chronon*) (208c). To satisfy this desire, people will do anything, even die (208c–d).[27] Individuals motivated by *philotimia* perform their marvelous deeds thinking that there will be an immortal memory of excellence about them (*oiomenous athanaton mnēmēn aretēs peri heautōn esesthai*) (208d5). Their desire, then, is for their personal participation in immortality through memory. Diotima says, at 208d7 and following, "I think that everyone does everything for the sake of immortal excellence (*aretēs*) and this sort of glorious reputation (*doxēs eukleous*), and by as much as they are better, by so much more do they do it. For they desire immortality (*tou athanatou*)." *Philotimia*, then, is the universal kind of human eros. Diotima notes that it is those who are better (*ameinous*) who most pursue excellence and glorious reputation, a claim that, at first glance, fits well with the archaic heroic ethos of death for glory manifested by Alcestis, Achilleus, and Codrus at 208d. This ethos is essentially an aristocratic one; the better (the elite) desire glory, while the worse (the lower classes) are motivated by desires characterized by the belly.[28] Diotima's linking of *hoi ameinous* and desire for glory also sits well with traditional Athenian elite ideology, which sees the elite as the better and as the group in Athenian society most concerned with excellence and honor. Diotima is clear, though, that *all* humans are driven by the eros that works itself out as *philotimia*. Manifestations of desire other than *philotimia*, then, would have to be imperfect forms of the universal desire.[29]

What distinguishes the desire of *hoi ameinous* from the desire of the not better is in what aspects of themselves they are pregnant, out of what aspect of themselves they will give birth in the beautiful, the body or the soul (208e–209a). Those pregnant in body produce children; those pregnant in soul produce wisdom and the rest of excellence (*phronēsin te kai tēn allēn aretēn*). What links the two manifestations of eros is that both are fulfilled in the production of something that perpetuates the lover past the limits of his own life. In children, Diotima says, people believe that they provide for themselves immortality, remembrance, and happiness into the whole future (208e). Those pregnant in soul produce poems that contain wisdom and excellence, technological products that manifest wisdom and excellence, and, best of all, wisdom about the proper running of cities and households (209a). These offspring, unlike the offspring of those pregnant in body, are themselves immortal (209c–d) and so carry with themselves into all future time the memory of their producers (209d). To be pregnant in soul and to give birth in the beautiful, then, is to produce something that is not dependent on reproduction for its participation in immortality. These offspring of the better lover, the lover pregnant in soul, live forever, not participating, it seems, in eros.

How is it, though, that these immortal offspring are in fact immortal? This question is not one that Diotima answers explicitly; she announces the fact of their immortality and then commences, at 210a, her account of the process by which the lover who is properly (*orthōs*) led by eros can come to see the beautiful and to know what the beautiful is (211c8–d1). Nonetheless, the answer to that question can be found in Diotima's account of how lovers pregnant in their souls give birth and in the story of the education of the lover by eros. What lies at the heart of these passages, for my purposes, is a notion of care and memory that is very much like the one I argued we see in Sappho's poems.

The one pregnant in soul, Diotima says, goes around seeking the beauty in which he will generate, being drawn to beautiful bodies more than to ugly ones and to the combination of a beautiful body with a beautiful, noble, and well-growing soul (*psuchēi kalēi kai gennaiai kai euphuei*) very much (209b2–7). With regards to *this* person (*pros touton ton anthrōpon*), the one who combines a beautiful body with a beautiful soul, the lover has an abundance (*euporei*) of *logoi* (notions, speeches, accounts) about excellence and about what the good man should be and what activities the good man must pursue; so the lover tries to educate the one with the beautiful body and beautiful soul (*epicheirei paideuein*) (209b7–c2). The lover is giving birth to ideas about excellence and about *how* to educate the man who is going to be good in generating *logoi* about what the good man should do and what the good man should be. The good man is, of course, the man who manifests excellence. The lover aims for his relationship with his beloved to transform the beloved, to secure the potential of the beloved's beautiful, noble, and well-growing soul. In the process of attempting the transformation of the beloved, the lover is himself changed; only in his relationship with *this* other person does he begin to have his abundance of *logoi* about excellence and education. His potential is also being secured by this relationship.[30] Further, what the lover has concerning excellence and education is *logoi:* words, speeches, accounts, and stories. This word, *logos,* covers a variety of meanings, linked by its relationship to the word *legein,* to say. In having *logoi* about excellence and education, the lover has *things to say* about excellence and education—he has things that exist to be communicated to another person. So the very thing that the lover gives birth to in the beauty of his beloved is a sharing (of experience) that presupposes a sharing (of language and all that goes along with language). He gives birth to a kind of *koinōnia,* an association, a having-in-common, a partnership. Moreover, the lover, with this beloved, commences a new relationship with the world; he moves out of adolescent virginity (he begins his search for the beauty that will allow him to give birth while still *neos* and *eitheos*) and moves into adulthood (*hēkousēs tēs hēlikias*) (209a8–b2). His arrival into adulthood is marked by his taking up the adult activity, education. This relationship is, then, transformative for both lover and beloved and serves, it seems, as a kind of rite of passage for the lover, at least.[31] The products of this relationship, *logoi,* are a sharing of understanding and value, since they are *logoi* about excellence and education.[32] This relationship, then, is from its outset reciprocal: lover and beloved together transform each other and bring into being together new *logoi* that neither of them would have without the other. Further, this relationship produces one of the things that make possible a relationship of care and commitment: an acknowledged sharing, an acknowledged communication.[33]

The lover, Diotima says, gives birth to and produces the things with which he long ago became pregnant by touching the beautiful one and passing time with him (*haptomenos . . . tou kalou kai homilōn autōi*), being mindful of him (*memnēmenos*) whether present or absent (209c2–4). Three activities, then, allow the lover to produce: touching the beloved, spending time with the beloved, and being mindful of or remembering the beloved.[34] Having given birth, the lover rears what he has produced in common with the beloved (*sunektrephei koinēi met' ekeinou*) (209c4). The relationship is not simply fulfilled by the production of *logoi* about excellence and education by the lover; rather, lover and beloved now become partners in a shared enterprise, the raising together to completion (*sun-ek-trephein*) of the *logoi.* Lover and beloved now share an object of care, their *logoi.*[35] The raising together to completion of *logoi,* presumably, involves a more thorough working-out of the *logoi* produced at first. Since it is a raising *together* of the *logoi,* then, this working-out should take the form of conversation, of shared participation in the working out together of the possibilities and implications of the initial *logoi.* Just as the relationship of lover and beloved begins as a relationship of reciprocal transformation, so it becomes, through their bringing up of their *logoi,* a relationship of shared responsibility to and transformation of these *logoi.*

The result of this situation of shared responsibility, Diotima tells us, is that lover and beloved share a greater community and a more secure *philia* (*meizō koinōnian . . . kai philian bebaioteran*) than exist between people who have produced children, since the offspring of lover and beloved are more beautiful and more immortal (209c5–7). Lover and beloved, because of their raising of their *logoi,* are now firmly joined together in sharing and *philia;* each recognizes the other as his own.[36] What has begun as eros, then, has revealed itself to be *philia*. Proper eros can result only in a relationship of reciprocal care and reciprocal responsibility. What secures this care and responsibility is the fact that the erotic relationship has from the beginning been productive and transformative. The lover, for *this* beloved, discovers himself with an abundance of things to say about what makes a man good, and he has shared those things to say with the beloved, wanting to educate him, wanting him to become a good man. The beloved, with *this* lover, has learned, has been able then to take up the project with his lover of developing these *logoi* about the good man. Through this joint effort, the two have become securely bound together by care.

What the lover saw in the beloved, the one who combines a beautiful body with a beautiful, noble, and well-growing soul was a *potential:* the potential, through education, to become a good man. His *own* potential became apparent to him in his desire for the beloved; he discovered himself to be someone who has things to say, someone capable of taking responsibility for another human being, someone capable of being efficacious in the world (remember that the lover in this account is himself quite a young man). Diotima does not tell us much about the beloved in the early stage of the relationship; what motivates him to accept this lover and his tutelage is not made explicit. Since the beloved has a beautiful, noble, and well-growing soul, it seems possible that what in turn draws him to this lover is a recognition of this lover as one who will be good for him, desirable because he will not be exploitative.[37] It is only when lover and beloved become partners in the rearing of the *logoi* that the beloved is portrayed by Diotima as being active in the relationship.[38] His activity is the activity that he shares with his lover, the raising together to completion of their *logoi*. The beloved himself is brought into adulthood by this relationship as he becomes a parent of *logoi*.

The offspring of the lovers are more beautiful and more immortal (*kallionōn kai athanatōterōn*) than regular children, with the result that the bond between the lovers is tighter and more secure than that between regular parents (209c5–7). As Diotima tells Socrates at 208b, what all human beings desire is immortality. *Logoi* better fulfill that desire because they are more immortal than children. They are also more beautiful, which means that they are themselves more likely to spur people to be productive of more *logoi,* since what we desire is giving birth in the *beautiful* and thereby participating in immortality.[39] Lover and beloved, then, feel themselves more fulfilled together in the raising of their *logoi* than they can feel in the production and raising of children. Since *logoi* are themselves beautiful and so inspirers of the production of new *logoi,* it should be the case that lover and beloved, in the raising of their *logoi,* produce ever more *logoi.* The *work* of their relationship, and, consequently, the satisfaction deriving from that work, should never end. The bond of the lovers is constantly renewing itself through their raising of their *logoi.*[40]

Diotima continues, "Everyone would welcome that such children (that is, *logoi*) have come to be, more than human ones, looking to Homer and envying (*zēlōn*) Hesiod and the other good poets the sort of offspring they have left behind for themselves, which provide for them immortal glory and memory (*kleos kai mnēmēn*) since they are themselves like that" (209c7–d3). What Homer, Hesiod, and the other good poets have produced is, of course, poems. These poems, still performed, heard, and read centuries after their production, have kept the names of their poets alive, have given their poets glory and memory.

Moreover, Diotima says that everyone is envious (*zēlōn*) of Hesiod and the other good poets. The use of this word in this context seems to allude to a passage early in Hesiod's poem *Works and Days.* In lines 11 to 26 of that poem, Hesiod explains that there are two kinds of strife (*eris*) among human beings, the destructive strife that causes disputes, lawsuits, and wars, and the productive strife that causes people, looking at (*idōn*) and being envious of (*zēloi*) their neighbors, to strive to be better at what they do. Cobbler strives against cobbler, farmer against farmer. This second strife is the strife of competition, which, Hesiod indicates, is what drives human beings to self-surpassing and excellence. (The second strife stirs up even the shiftless to work, makes people eager [*chatizei*] for work.) In the *Symposium,* then, we see that looking at and envying the good poets could itself lead to the production of good poetry, to more immortal offspring. Striving to surpass the accomplishments of those regarded by Greek culture as having been the good and the best poets is another motivation for the production of immortal *logoi.* The erotic relationship that Diotima describes seems, then, not to be the *only* path toward the production of *logoi,* poetic *logoi,* at least. Diotima suggests that, as the passage from *Works and Days* indicates, *eros* and *eris* are related compulsions that can achieve the same ends. She shows us also that we do not have to have an erotic relationship with another human being to produce *logoi.* Erotic activity (giving birth in the beautiful) is inspired by the *logoi* of the good poets that spur competition for immortal glory through the production of poetic *logoi.* The offspring of the good poets are, Diotima says, immortal. So, it turns out, are the offspring of Lycurgus, the lawgiver of the Spartans, and Solon, the lawgiver of the Athenians (209d4–7). What these two men produced were laws (*nomōn*) (209d8). Lycurgus is said to have developed the Spartan constitution that many Greeks felt was the source of the excellence, ethical, physical, and political, of the Spartan elite. Solon ended civil strife in Athens by developing a constitution that enfranchised more citizens and made wealth rather than family the factor that determined the extent to which a man could be involved in politics. The Lycurgan constitution was still in place in Sparta in the fifth and fourth centuries. The core laws of Solon's constitution likewise were still in effect in democratic Athens. Solon, Diotima says, is *timios* (held in honor) among the Athenians because of his production (*gennēsin*) of laws (209d6–7). Diotima goes on to say that other men in other places, among Greeks and barbarians, have produced all sorts of excellence and, for them, many temples (*hiera polla*) have been founded because of their offspring (209d7–e4). Great lawgivers are taken up into state religion in their cities; like Solon in Athens, they are *timioi*, held in honor.

Diotima's references in 209d–e to Homer, Hesiod, Lycurgus, Solon, and shrines indicate to us how it is that the offspring of these proper erotic relationships can be immortal: they are immortal because people, other than those who produced them, love them and care about them. The epics of Homer and Hesiod are immortal because Greeks continued to value them, study them, and perform them, and because they stand as examples of poetic success with which every new generation of poets could compete. This continued involvement has persisted until our own time. The constitutions of Lycurgus and Solon are immortal because the Spartans and the Athenians continued to govern themselves according to the laws they attributed to Lycurgus and Solon. Homeric and Hesiodic epic, the Lycurgan and Solonian constitutions, live as tradition. These *logoi* have become tradition because others took them up, saw in them things meaningful to them, lived with them, learned through them, and produced more *logoi* out of them. Others, over and over again, took these *logoi* as their own and so took responsibility for keeping these *logoi* active and successful in the world. Others took care that these *logoi* would in fact turn out to be immortal. That is, others have taken up these *logoi* as though they are themselves the producers of these *logoi* and have become groups of people who bring these *logoi* up to completion together (*sunektrephein*); the ones who first produced the *logoi* have given place to these new parent-lovers. These *logoi* have become a bond for groups—Greeks, Spartans, Athenians. These groups are held together by the same *philia* that ties lover and beloved in their rearing of their *logoi*, a *philia* that is constantly renewed by the recognition that we are all involved with those *logoi*, all committed to these *logoi*, all caring for these *logoi*.[41]

Eros

I have so far omitted from my discussions of Sappho and the *Symposium* any account of eros as a compulsive force. In the *Symposium*, by and large, this aspect of eros is not a primary concern of most of the speeches, with the exception of Aristophanes's and Alcibiades's speeches. Diotima's speech, which is my concern here, does not pursue this aspect of eros at any length. It is nonetheless the case, that, for Diotima, eros is a powerful force that drives people toward the beautiful, whether they wish to be driven or not, and in this regard, Diotima's notion of eros is in keeping with typical ancient Greek notions of compulsive eros. Some of the most famous articulations of *that* eros appear precisely among Sappho's fragments.[42] One question that must be addressed is how we are to reconcile this compulsive eros with the philosophical eros of care that Diotima articulates. That is the question that I will now answer.

There are three fragments of Sappho that are especially relevant here, 47, 130, and 16. I shall work through each of the fragments to draw out the different aspects of compulsive eros that Sappho explores.

> . . . and eros shook (*etinaxe*) my
> mind (*phrenas*), like a wind on a mountain falling on oak trees.
>   (fragment 47)

Eros here, first of all, is something that works on a person's mind (*phrenas*), shaking it. The verb that Sappho uses here, *etinaxe* (from *tinassō*), generally has the sense of holding an object in one's hand and shaking it. So the poet's mind is described here as physically under the control of an eros that holds it and moves it. The simile Sappho provides to explain the shaking of her mind by eros stresses that eros is outside of her mind; eros, like a wind falling on oak trees, falls on her mind. Just as trees cannot fail to be stirred by the wind in that they cannot resist its force, so eros here is a strong force that comes from outside and powerfully moves a person, regardless of whether the person wills it.

Fragment 130 tells us:

> Now again (*d'ēute*) eros the limb-loosener (*ho lusimelēs*) whirls
> (*donei*) me, sweet-bitter (*glukupikron*), unmanageable (*amachonon*),
> creeping (*orpeton*).

This fragment points first to the immediacy of desire; Sappho tells us that eros now again (*d'ēute*) whirls her. *D'ēute* is formed by crasis of two adverbs, *dē* (now, really) and *aute* (again). Eros has Sappho and eros has Sappho *now*. The poems remind us that desire can keep us absorbed in a now, mindful neither of past nor future.[43] Sappho calls eros here the limb-loosener. This adjective has two basic senses: that eros makes our limbs loose or relaxed and that eros detaches our limbs from us. Eros is limb-loosening in that it causes people not to be in firm, self-conscious control of their bodies, making them limp. Under the influence of eros, I am in some sense not attached to, not controlling, not immediately acting my will through my body. Eros is moving me, as we saw in fragment 47; here it whirls (*donei*) me. The verb here, *donei,* as with *etinaxe* in fragment 47, is transitive, denoting one thing causing another thing to whirl. Eros affects my body and, presumably, my thinking and feeling as well (as in fragment 47); being caught in the now by eros disorients and confuses me. Sappho describes eros in the second line of the fragment as sweet-bitter (*glukupikron*). Here she describes how it is one takes up, perceives, or interprets one's eros. It is a double thing, a sweet pleasure, but also sharp or bitter, a pain. It is moreover, *amachanon,* unmanageable, something against which there is no device (no *machana* or, in Attic, *mēchanē*). Eros cannot be dealt with. Once it has taken me, I have no recourse to any method, trick, or technological device; I am simply under its control. Finally, here, eros is creeping (*orpeton*). Here, Sappho portrays eros moving slowly and gently, rather than forcefully, as she does in fragment 47. Eros does not always take its hold suddenly and forcefully. Sometimes it takes hold slowly, without our noticing it until too late, at which point, again, we feel the impossible compulsion of desire. Fragments 47 and 130 show us an eros that is a force external to me, external to my will, that does as it pleases with me. In the grip of eros, I feel myself passive and helpless in the face of this thing that is moving me and which has taken away my independent self-determination.

What eros moves me toward is another human being. Sappho's fragment 16 tells how eros, the force that comes upon us from outside and sweetly compels us toward another person, also compels us not to be mindful of who we are independent of this eros. This poem tells us:

> Some say an army of horsemen, others an army of foot soldiers,
> and others an army of ships, is the most beautiful
> thing on the black earth, but *I* say it is
>   whatever someone loves (*eratai*);
>
> It is very easy to make this   5
> understood by everyone, for the one who by far surpassed
> humans in beauty, Helen, leaving behind
>   a husband very fine
>
> she went sailing to Troy
> and neither child nor dear (*philōn*) parents   10
> did she remember (*ouk emnasthē*) at all, but
>   . . .] led her astray.

Here Helen, loving Paris, abandoned her *life:* her marriage, her parents, her child. She turned her back on all the bonds of *philia;* she did not remember, was not mindful (*ouk emnasthē*) of those bonds. The bond that tied her to those who were her own was not strong enough to resist her eros for Paris. Helen lost, also, her social status, her relationships with the people and places she knew, and the future that she could have in that place with those people. In leaving behind her household, parents, husband, and child, she left behind her city, Sparta. Eros, then, has the capacity to force us to forget every aspect of ourselves, home and family life, our own people, and city and social identity. By keeping us always in the "now," eros detaches us from our own continuous life and existence within the rest of the world. Eros at its most forceful, then, stands *outside* the household and the city. It is essentially *wild.* It is a force of nature (*phusis*), of the world beyond the walls of house and city.[44]

I said earlier that Diotima, in her account of eros, does not address explicitly the compulsion of eros. It is nonetheless the case that this aspect of eros does appear in her discussion. As we have seen, Sappho's eros is a force that comes down on us from outside, driving us in one way or another. The force that Diotima's eros exerts, however, comes from *within* us—eros is part of our nature, our *phusis* (206c4; cf. 207a6–b4). Eros is part of what human beings are—part of how human beings grow, develop, and mature over time—as it is part of all animals (207a6 and following). All mortal nature (*phusis*) seeks as much as it can to be always and immortal, Diotima says (207d1–2). Thus, to feel desire is, for humans, part of the fabric of our being-in-the-world, like thinking or seeing. Our nature dictates that we must feel desire.

Even if eros is "ours" by nature, it is not something about which we have a choice. Eros comes to us when we mature sufficiently to feel it. Diotima notes that eros comes with maturity at 206c3–4, when she says, "our nature (*phusis*) desires to give birth whenever people come to be in some maturity (*en tini hēlikiai*)." Again, at 209a8–10 she says, "Whenever someone is pregnant in soul from youth, being unmarried and with maturity having come (*hēkousēs tēs hēlikias*), he now desires to give birth and reproduce." We *grow into* eros. I made no decision to develop breasts or to menstruate; in the same way I make no decision to begin to feel eros. All of these things are of my nature, of my growing.

One of the features of eros that Sappho stresses is that it in some way drives people out of their senses, confusing them and causing them to forget who they are. Diotima also acknowledges this effect of eros, developing her description of maddening eros first in an account of how it affects animals.[45] When animals are erotically disposed (*erōtikōs diatithemena*), they are sick (*nosounta*), first about mating and then about the rearing of their offspring, being ready to fight others stronger than themselves, to die for their off-spring, and to starve themselves so that they might feed their young (207a6–b5). Self-preservation, a fundamental instinct of all living things, is forgotten under eros; the conceiving, rearing, and preserving of the offspring are the dominant concerns of the erotically disposed animals.

Diotima gives a similar account of the behavior of humans motivated by *philotimia* at 208c:

> [These people] are in a terrible state (*deinōs diakeintai*) through an eros to become famous and to store up immortal glory for all time, and for the sake of this they are ready (*hetoimoi*) to run all risks still more than for children, and to spend money and to toil whatever types of toils and to die for it. (208c4–d2)

Philotimia, a universal type of human eros, puts people in a terrible state (*deinōs diakeintai*). Diotima uses the same words to describe animals at 206d8: "Do you not perceive what a terrible state (*hōs deinōs diatithetai*) all wild animals are in when they desire to produce?"[46] *Philotimia* causes people to forget self-preservation, it makes them ready to run risks, to die—again, Diotima uses the same word of animals: the weakest are ready (*hetoima*) even to fight for them (their offspring) against the strongest (206b3–4)—to forget about the preservation of the resources they have stored up, to spend money, and to exhaust themselves in toil. As Diotima describes it in these two passages, eros has the same effect on humans and animals: humans for the sake of a human goal and animals for the sake of an animal goal will forget themselves in their efforts to satisfy their eros. When she describes how erotically disposed animals behave, Diotima remarks, "Someone could think that human beings do these things out of reason (*ek logismou*)" (207b6–7). That is, we could think that human beings would die or starve for the sake of their children because they think they have a responsibility to these children or are aware that their immortality resides in their children and so act in particular ways to live up to that responsibility or to preserve that immortality. When she describes the behavior of people driven by *philotimia*, however, she says, "You would be amazed at the unreason (*tēs alogias*) if you don't keep in mind the things I have said [about eros]" (208c3–4). In considering the things that people are willing to do for the sake of becoming famous, one would have to think that these actions make no sense. Keeping in mind that they are motivated by the same desire that causes animals and people to die for their offspring, the desire to become immortal, we can see that they do make sense to the one who is thinking about them. The similarities in the two accounts of eros, animal and human, though, suggest that for both human and animal, the behavior that comes about because of the erotic disposition is not *ek logismou,* out of reason; for both, eros is a kind of madness marked by its ability to make us forget ourselves.

Eros and Memory

Diotima and Sappho, then, offer similar accounts of the effect of compulsive eros: it causes people to forget themselves. Sappho's image of eros falling down on her like a wind and Diotima's insistence that eros is a feature of all mortal nature both capture the unavoidable presence of eros; it is not something about which I can make a choice, either because it comes from outside of me and so is beyond my control or because it *is* me and so is beyond my control. In its effect on the desiring individual, then, and, as I argued earlier, in its necessary development into care, eros turns out to be much the same for Sappho and Diotima. A significant difference reveals itself, though, in what constitutes the object of eros. For Sappho, what I desire and, consequently, what I care for is another human being. For Diotima, this desire for another human being is only the beginning of eros, which, properly and philosophically developed, becomes desire and care for *logoi,* ideas, knowledge. This transformed eros, as I have argued, becomes, further, care for the group and for tradition.

Eros, then, initially a force of nature that, as Sappho articulates it, stands opposed to the bonds of *philia* between families and communities, when it is *educated,* manifested in the form that recognizes itself as a desire for immortality, becomes precisely a force that fosters care for community and for the institutions of community. Diotima herself acknowledges the wild side of eros when she remarks to Socrates that the uneducated eros that he and others feel for beautiful boys and young men drives them out of their wits (*ekpeplēxai*) and makes them ready (*hetoimoi*) to neither eat nor drink but to do nothing except look at them and be with them (211d2–8). This eros, marked again by what lovers are ready (*hetoimoi*) to do to satisfy it, drives lovers to become solely absorbed in the presence of the one beloved, abandoning all concern for every other aspect of life, even the most basic impulse toward self-preservation through nutrition. This eros separates lovers from everything but the beloved, keeps them absorbed in the now of their desire for this one beloved.[47] When eros leads a lover properly, however, when wild eros begins to become philosophical eros, the lover puts aside his "vehement gaping after one body" (*henos . . . to sphodra touto chalasai*) (210b5–6) and comes to desire excellence of soul, to see the beauty of laws and pursuits that foster this excellence, to see the beauty of knowledge, to see the beauty of knowing, and, at last, to see just what "beautiful" is (210b–e).[48] This eros is the one that stands at the core of the formation and maintenance of communities and their traditons.[49]

Philosophical eros, then, is eros that is committed first and foremost to *remembering*. The Greek verb *mimnēiskesthai*, to remember, means to be mindful of, aware of something. In poetic and ritual contexts, it has the sense of calling something from the past into a living present moment. For Sappho and Diotima, memory is a crucial aspect of eros and care. I am mindful of what I love, I keep it present to me, and I keep it present also to those around me. As Diotima's discussion of lover and beloved rearing their offspring, their *logoi*, together indicates, the immortality of these *logoi* depends upon people recognizing themselves as committed to the keeping alive of these *logoi*, the keeping in a living present of these poems, laws, ideas, and things to say that arose in the past—to the *remembering* of them. Eros is what keeps a people and its traditions alive.

It remains the case, however, that eros will always maintain its wild side. At the heart of Sappho's and Diotima's notions of eros and care always is the *I* that can stand apart from others—*my* desire, *my* care for *my* beloved at *this* moment, *my* immortality, *my* offspring, *my* logoi. Beside that *I* is the "now" that detaches us from the past and the future as we are gaping after what we desire. If we are to remember, the things that we remember must continue to be proper (*oikeion*) objects of care for *us*, they must continue to mean something to us, and they must be with us in our now. Memory, then, cannot manifest itself simply as a *preservation* of the old things intact; rather, it must take the form of our keeping things *alive*, actively meaningful and lovable in the present, and actively meaningful and lovable into the future.[50] And so, along with the preservation of the *logoi* must come what we see in Socrates's philosophical–erotic way of life, a continual reexamining of the *logoi* we have inherited, a questioning of our received world, our customs, our laws, our values, our beliefs. Out of this questioning, we can come to see the way in which we do love the tradition and the ways in which what we take up from the past allows us to keep living as the people that we are. The care that we manifest for tradition must also be care for *ourselves*, however. We must, as Socrates indicates in the *Apology* and as Diotima indicates in the *Symposium*, seek always for the *logoi* and practices that make people, including ourselves, good. Consequently, our caring memory must be a memory that is prepared to challenge and to transform what we have inherited so that it *can* make us now, in our world, good. Our tradition, kept alive through our living it, must be responsible to its own past, open always to the challenge of the present and to the possibility of its own self-transformation.

In this sense, Plato offers a thoroughly traditional taking up of the traditional eros, manifested so clearly in Sappho's poems: he acknowledges the wildness and compulsion of eros and sees in it also the possibility of transformation into a force for cultural and group unity. In articulating how it is that this move can take place, however, Plato transforms our understanding of our own erotic activity. What Diotima's speech in *Symposium* does is not to produce some new kind of eros that never existed in the world before Plato wrote the *Symposium,* but to reveal what was always implicitly the case about eros. Plato's text, in making explicit what it is we do when we love, when we compose poetry, when we make laws for ourselves, when we do philosophy, teaches us that our individual fulfillment, our projecting ourselves into the world and into the future, depends upon care for others, care for the self-fulfillment of others. He shows us, ultimately, that our erotic fulfillment must be both traditional and novel, responsible both to the traditions we have inherited and to the novel needs of our "now." This approach to tradition, simultaneously receptive and creative, is precisely what he himself enacts in his taking up of the traditional account of *eros* he inherited from Sappho.

PART II

Polis and Tradition

CHAPTER 3

Republic 3 and the Sirens

Diotima's account of eros in the *Symposium* reveals to us how tradition arises out of human desire for immortality and how eros is what keeps tradition alive, functional, and real to those who live within it. Socrates's transfiguring of the pederastic relationship in *Alcibiades* I conversely reveals how tradition gives form to desire by providing the parameters through which erotic relationships between human beings are enacted. This transfiguring takes place in *Alcibiades* I through precisely the kind of activity that Plato himself pursues in his reworking of received Greek notions of eros as the impulse behind philosophy and behind tradition as such: a careful, attentive, and critical rearticulation of the traditional that makes it alive and active as itself in a new situation. Socrates maintains the traditional structure and function of the pederastic relationship while shifting its focus to the beloved's attaining excellence. Plato maintains the traditional reciprocity and wildness of eros while shifting its focus to the arena of *logoi* and philosophy.

When we turn our attention to an *explicit* Socratic reworking of the traditional in Book 3 of the *Republic,* we find something quite different taking place. As in both *Alcibiades* I and Diotima's speech in the *Symposium,* what is at issue in the discussion that gives rise to the reworking of tradition is education. In *Republic* 3, Socrates and Glaucon are discussing the kind of education that the citizens in their new, purified city-in-thought will receive. The educational program of the new city will be typically Greek in that it will rest on the two planks of elite education, *mousikē* (music, poetry, and dance) and *gymnastikē* (athletics and physical training). *Mousikē* is the aspect of the new education that receives the most attention because it is through music, poetry, and dance that the citizens will learn about themselves, where they come from, what they value, and how they are to live together harmoniously. Socrates lays out the myths the new poetry will relate; in each case he adapts traditional material, material familiar to all Greeks, by expurgating from the stories any reference to strife among the gods.

What Socrates proposes to do in *Republic* 3 is not at all what we see in the transformations of tradition in *Alcibiades* I and *Symposium*. In *Republic* 3, Socrates makes a blanket claim of fact: the poets lie in their accounts of gods and heroes because they do not portray the gods and heroes as they are. He then goes on, in his retelling of the traditional material, to delete elements of the poets' accounts that appear inaccurate; in particular, he removes all references to strife between the gods, especially to strife between family members. He preserves those parts of the traditional material that will be *useful* for inculcating the values that he and Glaucon agree the new citizens should share. Their usefulness will rest in their being already *familiar* to the new citizens, all of whom will have grown up in a Greek city-state. What Socrates proposes, then, is not to adapt traditional material to a new context; keeping in mind what *Symposium* and *Alcibiades* I have shown us about tradition and its transformation, we know that it is those of us who live through and in the tradition who must adapt it for ourselves. Instead, what Socrates appears to do is to treat traditional material as merely instrumental, as merely a tool to be manipulated to complete a particular task, the formation of citizens through education. What *Republic* 3 reveals to us, though, is that the traditional material has a meaningful life of its own that reminds us repeatedly that Socrates's claims about these untraditional myths and their effects cannot be true.

So, the first step in the construction of the purified city in Book 3 of the *Republic* is the construction of its education.[1] Before the new citizens can go off to build their settlement, they, especially the rulers, must be prepared for their new world.[2] This education follows a typical Greek pattern of *mousikē* and *gymnastikē*. Once Socrates and Glaucon have worked out the models that the two planks of their education will follow, they discuss how these two elements, music and gymnastics, must be balanced; their new citizens must have neither too much nor too little of either if the souls of their citizens are not to fall into the extremes of savagery from too much gymnastics or softness from too much music (3.410d). This proper balance, they agree, is especially important in the guardians (410e).

At 411a–b, Socrates explains to Glaucon the effects of too much music on the soul. In this explanation, I will argue, Socrates alludes to the famous story of the Sirens from *Odyssey* 12. This allusion, we will see, does not ultimately serve the purpose that Socrates appears to claim for it. Rather than supporting the arguments about the model of education that Socrates makes—a model that rejects traditional authoritative portrayals of gods, heroes, and human beings in song—the allusion to the Sirens, by virtue of the meaning of the Sirens episode within the *Odyssey*, condemns Socrates's untraditional model of song. In what follows, I will first explain in what features of this

passage we can see an allusion to the Sirens episode. Here I will offer a substantial discussion of the Sirens episode to lay out just what that episode in
the *Odyssey* has to say about song, and, most importantly, about tradition
enshrined in song. Using what we learn from the Sirens about storytelling,
tradition, and human activity, I will examine Socrates's practice of storytelling as it relates to education in the purified city of *Republic* 3 and conclude
that, contrary to his own explicit claim that the traditional stories must be
censored, Socrates's stories in fact point to the need to embrace rather than
reject traditional poetry and artistic forms. I will conclude with an examination of the relationship between Socrates's myths, his city, and historical
Sparta, showing that Socrates is not in fact defending an ideal city-state, but
demonstrating the degeneracy of a city that presumes to manipulate traditional stories.

Republic 3 and *Odyssey* 12

At *Republic* 3.411a–b, Socrates says:

> When a man gives himself (*parechēi*) to music and lets the flute
> play and pour into his soul through his ears (*dia tōn ōtōn*), as it
> were into a funnel—using those sweet, soft, wailing harmonies
> (*tas glukeias te kai malakas kai thrēnōdeis harmonias*) we were just
> speaking of—and spends his whole life humming and exulting
> (*geganōmenos*) in song, at first, whatever spiritedness he had he
> softened (*emalaxe*) like iron and made useful from having been
> useless and hard. But when he keeps at it without letting up and
> charms his spirit (*kēlēi*), he, as the next step, already begins to melt
> (*tēkei*) and liquefy his spirit until he dissolves it completely (*heōs an
> ektēxēi ton thumon*) and cuts out, as it were, the sinews (*neura*) from
> his soul and makes it "a feeble warrior"(*malthakon aichmētēn*).[3]

This passage, as I will demonstrate, contains an extensive allusion to the Sirens of the *Odyssey*.[4] Rather than quote the Homeric passages entire, I will
summarize the narrative and then lay out the allusion. In *Odyssey* 12, Circe
gives advice to Odysseus about dealing with the obstacles he and his companions will meet on their way home. The first problem, Circe says, will be
the Sirens, who enchant everyone who hears their singing. No one who hears
their song gets a homecoming; the Sirens are surrounded by a pile of bones
and rotting skin from the ones who have heard them. She advises Odysseus
to plug his companions' ears with wax so that they will not hear the Sirens. If

Odysseus himself wants to listen and enjoy the song, he should have himself tied to the mast so that he cannot escape his ship (*Odyssey* 12.37–54). When Odysseus and his companions approach the Sirens' island, he plugs the crew's ears with wax and they bind him to the mast. The Sirens sing to Odysseus, attempting to persuade him to stop the ship and listen to them. Odysseus longs to hear them and signals his companions to release him. Two of them tighten his bonds, and they continue their journey until they are out of range of the Sirens' voices (12.165–200).

The allusion here is not as obvious as some of Socrates's other allusions in Book 3, such as the reference to the myth of the five races of human beings from Hesiod's *Works and Days* at 415a–b. Nonetheless, as we will see, the reference in Plato's text is extensive and carefully worked out.[5] Note, first of all, the situation of the man excessively devoted to music and the situation of Odysseus: both give themselves to music.[6] Odysseus gets himself tied to the mast for the sole purpose of listening to the Sirens; Circe tells him he should tie himself to the mast if he wants to hear their song, and he tells his companions that Circe told him alone to hear the Sirens, so they should bind him to the mast. Next, both the *Republic* passage and the *Odyssey* passages stress the perception of song through the ears: music enters the soul "through the ears" at *Republic* 411a3 and the ears of the companions are plugged to prevent their hearing the Sirens at *Odyssey* 12.47 to 48 and 173 to 177.

Socrates next characterizes the harmonies of the overly musical man as sweet, soft, and wailing (*glukeiai, malakai, thrēnōdeis*). The Sirens at 12.187 claim their voice is *meligērus*, honey-voiced, and so sweet and soft; this adjective appears only here in the Homeric poems, but "honey-" compounds typically are used for things that are sweet, like wine, or soft and gentle, like fresh grass or sleep. The harmonies here are also *thrēnōdeis*, like a funeral dirge. The song of the Sirens in *Odyssey* 12 is not a funerary lament, but a song that brings about the deaths of those who hear it.[7] Moreover, the Sirens have long associations in Greece with graves and tombs.[8] So sweetness, softness, and death pertain to Socrates's music and to the Sirens' song.

The musical man passes his life humming and rejoicing in song, *geganō-menos*. This verb, *ganaō*, has a cognate that appears at *Odyssey* 12.43, where Circe says the wife and children of the man who hears the Sirens will not rejoice, *ganuntai*, in him after he gets home. We also see, 12.52, *terpomenos*, taking pleasure, to describe Odysseus's response to the Sirens. Again, in both passages, we see explicit appeals to notions of pleasure and delight, with overlapping diction.

The first effect of music on the spirit, Socrates says, is to soften it and to make it useful.[9] In the *Odyssey*, Circe tells Odysseus to soften wax to put into his companions' ears, and later the wax grows soft in the sun. The Sirens, further, claim that those who hear their song go home knowing more things (12.188), claiming a kind of utility for their song.

When the overly musical man keeps on listening to music, he is enchanted by a spell, *kēlēi*, 411b. The Sirens also enchant; they *thelgousin* at 12.40 and 44. Once the man has been enchanted, he melts his spirit until he melts it completely away—*tēkei . . . heōs an ektēxēi ton thumon*. Note that Plato uses *tēkō* twice here for "melt." This verb and its compounds are relatively uncommon in the Homeric poems, but they have a marked use. They appear nine times in total, eight times in the *Odyssey*, once in the *Iliad*.[10] This verb appears consistently in contexts in which a person weeps for one of his or her *philoi* (kin or friends), having been reminded of the past through some form of storytelling. In the *Odyssey*, in particular, the verb occurs regularly in passages in which Odysseus himself is the subject of the verb *or* the motivator of the melting. In a Homeric context, then, this verb means something like "to melt (into tears) in response to a story about one's *philoi*."[11] One of the uses, at 19.264, has the verb take *thumos* as its direct object, as in the *Republic* passage (*ektēxēi ton thumon*), when the disguised Odysseus tells Penelope not to melt away her spirit lamenting her husband (*mēde ti thumon / tēke posin gooōsa*). *Tēkō* is the Homeric tradition's verb for sorrow, *philia*, and storytelling. The *Republic* passage uses a marked Homeric word here to describe, as the *Odyssey* itself does, one of the effects of song and storytelling.

The musical man, Socrates continues, melts away his spirit and cuts it out just like sinews from his soul. Our *Odyssey* passage refers to body parts also, to the bones and skin of the rotting men (12.45–46). Without his spirit, the man becomes a feeble warrior, a *malthakos aichmētēs*. This tag is Homeric, occurring only once, and in the *Iliad*, at 17.588, where Apollo asks Hektor why he trembles now at Menelaos, who previously was a *malthakos aichmētēs*. Plato closes this description of what too much music can do by flagging the Homeric nature of what has been discussed.

In this passage, Plato ties Socrates's portrayal of the man excessively devoted to music subtly and thoroughly to the portrayal of the Sirens in the *Odyssey*. The imagery and themes draw heavily, but never explicitly, on the *Odyssey* passages. Plato here is inviting the well-informed reader, the reader who knows the poems that lie at the heart of traditional Greek *mousikē*, to remember the Sirens as Socrates talks about what music in itself does to people. Plato invites us to remember what the Homeric Sirens have to tell us about *song*.[12]

There are many things to learn about song from the Sirens. I will focus here on what I take to be the most salient feature, which is the lack of authority and tradition in the Sirens' song. The Sirens give the appearance of singing within the appropriately authorized song tradition, but they do not, and, consequently, their song is both deceitful and destructive. Let us begin by looking at the words the Sirens sing at *Odyssey* 12.184–91.

> Come here as you go, much-praised (*poluainos*) Odysseus,
>   great glory of the Achaeans (*mega kudos Achaiōn*),
> beach your ship, so that you may hear the voice of us two.   185
> For not yet has someone driven past in his black ship,
> before he hears the honey-speaking voice from our mouths,
> but, having taken pleasure, he goes home knowing even more
>   things.
> For, you know, we know all things, as many as in broad Troy
> the Argives and Trojans struggled by the will of the gods;   190
> and we know as many things as happen upon the much-
>   nurturing earth.

I note first that the Sirens demonstrate and claim here an omniscience comparable to that of the Homeric Muses. At line 184, they address Odysseus by name and apply two traditional epithets to him, indicating that they recognize him and know the songs about him. They state further that they know not only the entire Troy cycle (the things the Argives and Trojans struggled over in Troy at lines 189–190) but also everything on earth (line 191). This knowledge of all things is most famously attributed to the Muses in Book 2 of the *Iliad,* where the singer invokes them just prior to commencing the Catalog of Ships (*Iliad* 2.484–87). He says:

> Tell now to me, Muses having Olympian homes—
> for you are goddesses, and you are present, and you know
>   everything,
> but we only hear the glory and we don't know anything—
> whoever were the leaders and chiefs of the Danaans.

The Sirens, then, invite comparison with the Muses. To understand what this comparison means, I will examine the most significant way in which the Sirens are *not* like the Muses: the Sirens lack the traditional song authority of the Muses and the traditional Homeric markers of authoritative human speech. The absence of traditional authority itself marks the Sirens' song as one to be rejected by the Homeric audience.

The Muses are the patrons of the epic singer, invoked at the beginning of a poem and at important moments within the epic narrative to strengthen and inform the singer, as in the invocation from *Iliad* 2 quoted above. The Muses are also, within divine society, performers of song. Their precise performance role in the divine sphere is what allows their authority over human song. We see the Muses perform at the close of *Iliad* 1 at a banquet of the gods on Olympus. Here the Muses sing while Apollo accompanies them on the lyre (*Iliad* 1.601–4):

> Thus they feasted for the whole day until the setting
> of the sun, nor was their spirit lacking at all in the equal feast,
> nor in the exceedingly beautiful lyre that Apollo was holding,
> and not in the Muses, who were singing in response to each other
>   with their beautiful voice.

In this passage, the poem shows us the Muses performing as a chorus whose *chorēgos,* chorus leader, is Apollo. We see a similar situation portrayed outside epic in Pindar's fifth Nemean ode, where the Muses and Apollo perform at the wedding of Peleus and Thetis, the parents of Achilleus. Here (*Nemea* 5.41–45):

> Eager the very beautiful chorus of Muses sang
> for them on Pelion, and in the middle of them
> Apollo, striking the seven-tongued
> lyre with his golden plectrum
> leads them in all sorts of melodies.   45

In this passage, the Muses form a circular chorus at whose center Apollo accompanies and *leads* their performance.

Claude Calame, in a study of the Archaic Greek chorus, *Les choeurs de jeunes filles en Grèce archaïque,* has explained the role and function of the chorus leader, the *chorēgos.*[13] The *chorēgos,* often by accompanying the chorus instrumentally, starts the chorus's song and sets the rhythm and the pitch. The *chorēgos,* moreover, is always set off from the other members of the chorus, marked by more ornate costuming and possessing a higher social status. In the passages from *Iliad* 1 and *Nemea* 5, we see Apollo, distinguished from the Muses by being male and a major Olympian god, positioned in *Nemea* 5 at the center of their chorus, leading their song while accompanying them with his lyre. Apollo, god of the lyre, preeminent god of song, takes charge of the chorus of Muses and directs this chorus by his own authority.

The Muses are also gods of song, which is the feature that allows them to provide inspiration for human song, as they do at the beginning of both the *Iliad* and the *Odyssey*. They possess this authority because Apollo, the god who subsumes all song under his authority, shares it with them. This type of delegation is typical of all divine spheres of influence in Archaic Greek myth and poetry, in which everything is controlled by Zeus, who delegates authority and responsibility to the other gods. The Muses can take the role of *chorēgos* for larger choruses, as they do in the *Homeric Hymn to Apollo*, 188 to 196, where they sing so that other goddesses can dance. We see the Muses as *chorēgos* in Pindar's first Pythian ode (lines 1–4), where the Muses lead human choruses. As members of the chorus of Apollo, the *chorēgos* par excellence, the Muses sing by and through his authority and partake of that authority in their domain over other singers.

The Sirens of the *Odyssey*, however, sing by no one's authority but their own. They have no chorus leader to direct their song and no Muse to inspire and inform it. They introduce themselves to Odysseus simply by singing and promising him pleasure and knowledge. The Sirens invoke no Muse, and they do not identify themselves; they offer only *their own* song and *their own* knowledge. The Sirens' song lacks the traditional authority of the chorus, an authority the Muses possess, and the authority of the inspiration of the Muses, an authority a human singer possesses.

In Homeric epic, another factor in determining whether or not song is possessed of authority and is to be listened to is knowledge. As we saw in the invocation of the Muses prior to the Catalog of Ships, the Muses provide the singer with the resources to sing his song. Because they are goddesses, are present, and know all things, they can tell the singer the right things to say. The singer gets the strength and the accurate knowledge to sing the Catalog of Ships from the Muses. He says:

> I would not tell their number nor would I name it
> not even if I had ten tongues, and ten mouths,
> and an unbreakable voice, and the heart in me was bronze,   490
> unless the Olympian Muses, daughters of Zeus
> aegis-holder, reminded me how many came beneath Ilion.
> (Iliad 2.488–92)

Every time the singer wants to ensure his accuracy, to show that he has the right information in his song, he calls upon the Muses for assistance. So, at the *end* of the Catalog of Ships, he asks the Muse to tell him which men and horses were best (2.761–62). We see three more invocations in the *Iliad*, all of which request information. In Book 11, the singer asks which Trojan first came forth to fight Agamemnon. In Book 14, he asks which Achaean made the first kill after Poseidon entered battle, and in Book 16 he asks how fire first came to the ships of the Achaeans. When a particularly important point in the narrative comes, the singer calls on the knowledge and memory of the Muses to show that *his* words are the right words, validated by the traditional authority vested in the Muses.

As I noted earlier when I quoted the Sirens' song from *Odyssey* 12, the Sirens make a claim to a similar kind of authority for themselves: they claim to be omniscient. As Odysseus sails past, the Sirens call out to him, telling him they know all that happened at Troy and everything that happens on earth (12.189–90). But they give no account of where they get this knowledge. They do not claim to have been present at things the way the Muses are present, nor do they say they sing with the help of Apollo or the Muses. The Muses are the daughters of Zeus and Mnemosyne, Memory, and, as the ones who remind the poet what to sing, they embody the authority of tradition, of the memory of a culture.[14] The Sirens have no pedigree at all; neither they, Circe, nor Odysseus mention a family line or a concrete past for them. The Sirens are, then, unknown in a context where ties to the past through the father's line were of paramount importance.[15] They consequently lack another Homeric mark of authority in speech, reputation.[16] Because they have no status and no recognizable place in the world to make them knowable, their song does not demand to be heard.[17] Neither Odysseus nor, by extension, the *Odyssey*'s audience, needs to hear this song.

To say that no one needs to hear their song because the Sirens lack traditional authority is, of course, not the same as to say that their song must be rejected because it is dangerous. The danger of the song lies in its content, in what the Sirens promise to sing for Odysseus. The Sirens address Odysseus with two epithets that state his role as already part of song tradition because of his exploits at Troy: they call him *poluainos*, much-praised, and *mega kudos Achaiōn*, great glory of the Achaeans (12.184). The Sirens address Odysseus, not as the hero he now is, the hero of the *Odyssey*, but as the hero he was in the *Iliad*. The epithets they use to address him, in addition to marking Odysseus as someone about whom song is performed, are specifically *Iliadic* epithets. *Poluainos* appears three times in the *Iliad*, each time for Odysseus (and only in the present passage in the *Odyssey*, again for Odysseus).[18] *Mega kudos Achaiōn* appears in the *Iliad* twice for Odysseus (once for Odysseus, in the present passage, in the *Odyssey*)[19] and four times for Nestor[20] (twice for

Nestor in the *Odyssey*).[21] The Sirens also pointedly tell Odysseus that they know about the Trojan War, as an indicator of what they are going to sing for him. The Sirens, then, offer to sing some version of the *Iliad*.[22]

So the Sirens give the appearance of presenting a traditional epic song. Their own lack of traditional signs of authority already undermines this appearance of traditionality. There is a set of epithets used for Odysseus in the *Iliad* that is clearly distinguished from the epithets used for him in the *Odyssey;* the Sirens' use of Iliadic epithets calls their adherence to the tradition further into question. Their misuse of these traditional elements in this instance goes hand-in-hand with what appears to be the Sirens' general use of song: they do it at the wrong time. The time for song, well-established by song practice within the *Iliad* and *Odyssey,* is the time of *leisure* and festivity. For example, when Odysseus hears Trojan War song in the court of the Phaeacians in *Odyssey* 8, there is nothing problematic taking place. Demodocus the singer is loved by the Muses and sings with appropriate inspiration from them (8.63–64). The context is one of festivity and rest; the work of preparing to take Odysseus home has been completed, and so now a feast and some songs are prepared (8.34–35). This setting of labor completed and restfulness does not at all pertain in the Sirens episode.

The Sirens sing to people engaged in work of some kind, in the work of sailing. Odysseus is engaged not merely in the work of sailing from one place to another, but in the *poem*'s work—he is trying to achieve homecoming, *nostos*. Odysseus's struggle to achieve homecoming is the stated theme of the *Odyssey* (1.5). The Sirens' song attempts to interfere with a goal shared by the poem and its hero. The Sirens offer Odysseus a chance to yield to the pleasure of hearing his own glory in hearing the story of his own past. They ask him to stop what he is doing so that he can hear this song. Odysseus must at this time move forward and continue the struggle to achieve *nostos* for himself and his companions. What the Sirens offer Odysseus is the pleasure of nostalgia, of hearing his own story, of weeping over it, as he does over Demodocus's song of the Trojan Horse in *Odyssey* 8, and of taking pleasure in that weeping, as he does in *Odyssey* 9. Odysseus cannot yield to this nostalgic pleasure in Book 12 if he is going to get home, if he is going to have a future as well as a past, and if he is going to achieve the kind of glory that interests the *Odyssey,* the glory of successful homecoming.

This episode tells us something about song and tradition. Song is the foundation of cultural identity for the Greeks, especially mythic song, especially retelling of traditional stories in traditional diction in traditional contexts, as we see in epic performance.[23] Tradition enshrined in song is how a group tells itself and the individuals upon whom it depends who it is, what is important to it, and what it believes. Tradition is an institution that provides the possibility of a future that is continuous with the past and the present—that is an organic living movement ahead. Song tradition at the level of the group serves much the same function as *nostos* does for the individual. (This is one of the reasons that Socrates discusses song first in his account of education in *Republic* 3.) In the *Odyssey*, Odysseus's *nostos* is not the reaching of a place, but the learning *who he is* and *what this place is*. Both *nostos* and tradition involve being who you are and knowing who you are so that you can keep going.

Anyone who hears the Sirens gets neither *nostos* nor tradition. The Sirens *lie,* telling Odysseus that the one who hears them goes home knowing more things after taking pleasure in their voice. The Sirens lie to prevent Odysseus's return home. They pervert the traditional function of song as purveyor of identity, fosterer of movement. The Sirens create a world in which song causes immobility and death. They are enemies to human tradition.

So when Plato alludes to the Sirens at 411a–b, he alludes *not* to the effects of music as such, but to the effects of song *without tradition* upon its listeners. This type of song kills everyone who hears it. This allusion alerts us, the readers who know the tradition, to the dangers posed by Socrates's versions of the traditional stories. He, like the Sirens, pretends to adhere to traditional standards, to purvey traditional material in a way that is appropriate for its context, the education of the guardians in true beliefs about gods, heroes, and human beings. But Socrates, like the Sirens, is lying, and Plato invites us, through the warning provided by this allusion, to scrutinize very carefully Socrates's appeals to traditional song material.

Socrates's Foundational Myths

Next I will examine the three "foundation" myths Socrates uses. The first of these is from *Republic* Book 2; it is the first myth Socrates rejects in his development of education, the Hesiodic story of Ouranus, Cronus, and Zeus at 2.377e–378a. This story is foundational here to the extent that it provides the model for all of Socrates's subsequent treatment of earlier song. Next I will look at the foundation myths of the new city at 3.414c–415c. Here Socrates reworks, first, stories of the earth-born men from the myths of Cadmus and Jason and then the Hesiodic five ages of humans from the *Works and Days*. Heeding the warning offered by the allusion to the Sirens, we will see that each of Socrates's retellings of traditional tales in his untraditional way points to serious problems inherent in the city Socrates is founding. The tradition lets us know how Socrates's innovation has to fail.

The music (*mousikē*) in Socrates's new city is defined, on the whole, negatively. Socrates proposes to continue to use traditional material, but to remove those aspects or genres that do not seem to support the development of good citizens. Socrates states, at the beginning of his account of the new music, what types of stories will be told—that the problem with the stories that Hesiod, Homer, and the other poets tell is that the tales in no way represent gods and heroes as they are (2.377d–e). So the first story that must be rejected is Hesiod's lie about how Ouranus did the things Hesiod says he did, how Cronus took vengeance upon him, and the deeds and sufferings of Cronus at the hands of his son (377e–378a). Socrates refers here to the succession myth from Hesiod's *Theogony*. His presentation is brief and seems straightforward. To teach the new citizens to honor the gods and each other, all reference to divine misbehavior, especially here to violence toward kin, must be kept out of education. Socrates *gestures* here toward the *kind* of thing we do not want our new citizens to hear and then moves on.[24]

But Socrates is drawing to our attention to one of the most ancient and well-known poems of the Greeks, the *Theogony*, and to the core of that poem's narrative and themes. So we are reminded of the story that Hesiod tells, and notice that Socrates reasonably omits much detail from his brief reference. I will summarize the story briefly. Ouranus, Heaven, consort of Gaea, Earth, does not want their offspring to survive, so he puts all of their children back into Gaea. Gaea grows angry, devises a plot, and approaches Cronus to assist her in getting vengeance upon his father. Cronus castrates Ouranus and becomes the ruler of the cosmos. He fears usurpation by one of his own sons, so he swallows all the offspring his consort Rhea bears. When Rhea is pregnant with Zeus, she enlists the help of Gaea and Ouranus to devise a plan to save Zeus and get vengeance for Ouranus and all of Rhea's children by Cronus. Rhea gives Cronus a stone to swallow, Gaea rears Zeus in secret, and Gaea deceives Cronus into disgorging all of his children. Zeus and his siblings go to war with Cronus and his generation and fight for a long time. Gaea advises Zeus to release her offspring the hundred-handers to help Zeus and his siblings against the Titans.

Notice here that, as Hesiod tells this story, the prime mover of vengeance against and usurpation of the father is *not* the son, but the mother. Note also that Gaea/Earth is the essential deviser of plans and provider of advice, even against her own son and one-time ally Cronus. The elements of *Theogony* narrative Socrates omits here point to, first, the violence inherent in the earth-born (Cronus and the Titans, the hundred-handers) and to the earth-mother's unceasing hostility to any present ruler. Gaea aids in the overthrow first of her son-consort Ouranus and then in the overthrow of her son Cronus. Gaea proves dangerous to Zeus as well because, after Zeus is established as ruler of the gods, Gaea brings forth her last child, Typhoeus, who challenges Zeus unsuccessfully. In this instance, the *Theogony* does not mention any hostile intent on Gaea's part when she produces this son that challenges Zeus. This absence of intent makes even more pointed the simple inherent danger to authority of the earth-born, and of the earth-mother.

These aspects of the omitted material do not seem immediately all that important in the context in which Socrates mentions the *Theogony*. His point is that stories about divine strife must not be told, and the *Theogony* certainly does tell a story of divine strife.[25] However, this succession myth, with Socrates's omission of the role of the mother, especially Gaea, in the overthrow of rulers, looks ahead to another one of Socrates's myths, where again the earth-mother figure plays a role.

Socrates and Glaucon discuss at 412b to 414b how, once all their young men get educated, they will decide who is to be the ruler and who the ruled. The best guardian will be the one who loves the city (the verb here is *phileō*, whose basic meaning, as we saw in chapter 1, is "to regard as one's own") (412d) and who does what is good for the city (412e). All of the citizens will of course have to love the city, and Socrates proposes, at 414c, that they need to come up with some way to persuade the citizens to love the city. He suggests that they devise their own story (414d–415e) to encourage the beliefs about the city Socrates wants to foster.[26]

Socrates introduces his story by calling it, first, a noble lie (414c) and next a Phoenician something (414c), that "has already happened in many places before, as the poets assert and have caused others to believe."[27] Socrates suggests coming up with, not just a story, but a *myth*. A myth is a story, but a special kind of story—it is a traditional tale used by a culture to tell itself what it believes and what it values. The ancient Greeks did not use their word *muthos* (the source of our word *myth*) in this sense. A *muthos* is a story or even a word—a lie, a historical narrative, and a hello are all *muthoi*. When Plato refers *unambiguously* to what we now call myth, he calls it "what the poets say."[28] So here, when Socrates says that they must come up with something that the poets assert, he is saying that they will come up with a myth. This story they come up with, further, will not just be told to the first generation of citizens, it will be told to "their sons and their successors and the rest of the human beings who come afterward" (415d), who will believe it.[29] This new story will become *traditional* and be handed down from one generation to the next. So Socrates and Glaucon here are inventing what they hope will be a traditional tale used by their city to tell itself what it believes. They are inventing what we call a myth.[30]

When we examine the content of this myth we see that Socrates does not create something entirely novel, as he himself notes when he says that they will tell nothing new at 414c. He recycles traditional material to serve as the myth of his city's origins.[31] The first element of the new foundation will tell the citizens that they were born out of the earth fully armed (414d–e); they were crafted under the earth along with their arms and other tools, and when they were all finished off, the earth, their mother, sent them forth. Socrates appeals here to two well-known stories about men being born fully armed from the earth. These are part of the Cadmus myth and of the myth of Jason and the Argonauts. The relevant section of each version of the story goes roughly as follows: the hero sows some serpent's teeth into the earth. From the teeth grow armed warriors. The hero throws a stone amongst the warriors, who immediately turn upon one another and fight. In the Cadmus myth, all of the warriors kill one another, except for five who join Cadmus in founding Thebes. In the Jason myth, all of the warriors die.[32] Socrates claims that his new myth will encourage the citizens to tend the city like a mother and to regard all fellow-citizens as brothers and earth-born, *gēgenēs* (414e). This myth should foster peaceful unity within the city and fierce defense of her from outside attack.[33]

The traditional material tells another story. It tells us that the nature of the earth-born is to engage in violent mutual destruction. Earth-born humans are no different from the earth-born gods of the *Theogony* we examined earlier. Socrates again omits parts of his traditional material. Again the traditional material reminds us that things are not as Socrates claims. Socrates's use of the notion of the earth-born points to an innate instability in his new city. These citizens will destroy one another.[34] The second myth Socrates proposes explains why these new citizens will indeed be mutually destructive.

The next plank in Socrates's invention of myth will tell citizens that, as the god was shaping them, he mixed various metals into them: gold into those who can rule, silver into the auxiliaries, and iron and bronze into the farmers and the other craftsmen (415a). The value of each metal corresponds to social status. In this passage, Socrates reworks the myth of the five races of humans from Hesiod's *Works and Days*. Here Hesiod describes how the gods populated the earth with a series of five races of people, the gold, the silver, the bronze, the heroic, and the iron (*Works and Days* 109–201). The gold race dies off, the gods destroy the silver race, the bronze race kills itself in battle, the heroic race either kills itself in battle or is removed to the Isles of the Blessed, and the iron race is our present race, which Zeus will destroy when "father will not agree with his children nor children with father, nor guest with host, nor companion with companion, and brother will not be *philos* [regarded as his own] to brother as before" (182–84). The last race, our race, will perish when ties of *philia* (the regarding of others as one's own) no longer bind us. The prime tie of *philia* is that between blood kin, as with fathers and children, brother and brother.

Socrates's myth of metals here is to be used to justify parents rejecting children who are not of their metal (415b–c). A gold parent can produce a silver child or a bronze parent a gold one; when this happens, the parents must send the child away to its appropriate metallic place. In the purified city, then, elevation and degradation of citizens will be commonplace. The citizens will take this responsibility especially seriously because they will believe that there is an oracle saying the city will be destroyed when an iron or bronze man serves as its guardian (415c–d).

Socrates's reworking of the traditional material again reminds us of aspects of the traditional material that call into question his explicit claims. Socrates departs significantly from the Hesiodic model here in that his races all exist at the same time, whereas Hesiod's races come one after another over time. Socrates's myth does not give his people a past; it marks them as *innovations*. These citizens, having no cultural past, will be able easily to do the very thing that, in the *Works and Days,* will bring about the destruction of the iron race: they will be able to disregard the *philia* of kin ties.[35] Socrates hopes to displace the *philia* of kin ties onto fellow citizens or onto the city itself. Those who know the myth of the five ages of humans know that displacement of kin ties, in that myth, leads to self-destruction, and any ancient Greek outside Sparta would know that this displacement is impossible and the demand for displacement excessive.[36]

Once again, the traditional material provides an account at odds with Socrates's stated goals. The myth of the metallic races does not teach us to disregard kin ties; it reminds us that kin ties are the foundation of *philia* and that without *philia* no human society is possible.[37] Socrates himself recognizes the integral necessity of kin-*philia* for founding his city when he constructs his myth of the earth-mother to inspire kinship-like *philia* among his citizens.[38] Nonetheless, the city will depend for its function on complete rejection of kin-*philia* when it demands, in Book 5 (458c–462a), the holding of children in common.

Socrates's foundation myths can be seen to follow the model of the Sirens from *Odyssey* 12. These "songs" all give the appearance of resting on traditional foundations and of purveying traditional material. The Sirens seem to know the *Iliad,* Socrates seems to draw on Hesiodic myths and myths of the earth-born. They are all pleasant to listen to. Odysseus will be pleased by the Sirens, young men enjoy talking with Socrates, and we enjoy reading those conversations. The pleasure, though, can distract us from what is going on. While we enjoy the Sirens' song, we are dying on the beach. While we enjoy Socrates, we may be overlooking that he is using mythical *exempla* that serve to foreshadow the self-destruction of the city in words.[39] These two myths, further, direct us ahead to the building of the city and the laying out of its basic laws at 415d to the end of Book 3 at 417b.

This new city, it emerges, will begin, not as a city in itself, but as a camp within a city (415a); the rulers, supported by the earth-born men, will control those within the camp and ward off attack from the outside (415d–e). In this camp, the guardians will be provided with housing and other necessities by the citizens (416c–d); the guardians will have no private property; fellow-citizens will provide the guardians with food appropriate to soldiers; the guardians will eat regularly in common messes (*xussitia*) and live a shared life; the guardians will be forbidden by law to possess gold or silver; and the guardians will not engage in activities involving the acquisition of profit (416e–417a). This new city will be, as is generally recognized, a Sparta.

Republic 3 and Sparta

Socrates's account of the life of the guardians at the end of *Republic* 3 depicts an elite group that resembles in several ways the elite male citizen group in historical Sparta, the Spartiatae. Sparta within Laconia was by and large a military camp on constant alert against rebellion from within from the serfs, or helots. Within the military camp, elite citizen men dominated the rest of the population and were supported by the labor of an oppressed majority. The Spartan educational system for citizen men, the *agogē*, enforced a transference of kin-*philia* to the city and to the male citizen group; crucial to the success of this enforcement was sending the male children to live in common barracks at the age of seven. The Spartiatae, further, ate a notoriously frugal diet and took their meals in common messes (*sussitia*). Spartiatae were forbidden to use currency or to engage in trade. They were also liable to degradation from full citizen status for various kinds of failure to meet the minimum standards of Spartiate rank.[40]

The similarities between historical Sparta and our city in words are fairly apparent. Socrates's account of "Sparta" here is idealizing, stressing features that many Greeks, including many Athenians, found appealing.[41] His two foundation myths, though, remind us of other sides of Sparta. The myth of the earth-born alludes to the earth-born who helped to found Thebes.[42] These earth-born were referred to as the Sown Men, the *Spartoi*. *Spartoi* and Sparta have no etymological or mythic connection, but there is a punning connection on which Plato draws here. So Socrates, alluding to *Spartoi*, is potentially alluding to Sparta, whose presence he invokes only moments later. The Spartoi are remarkable for their violent self-destruction; the ruling class of Sparta, the Spartiates, were obsessed as a group with their own violent destruction by the lower classes of Lacedaemon, with some justification. The lowest class, the helots, rebelled whenever possible.

The myth of the races, with its undermining of kin-*philia*, points to the education of the Spartan elite's male children by first driving them out of the mother's household, and later driving them out of the city to survive in the countryside without support. Young Spartiate men, further, lived in the common barracks, under the authority of a city magistrate, the paid-onomos, until they were thirty years old, even after marriage. Married men under thirty were forbidden to be seen entering or leaving their wives' homes. Citizen children, then, could be several years old before they even saw their fathers. The full citizen male was to have no attachment to other males of his own bloodline and minimal attachment to the females. The objects of affection and commitment were the male citizen group and the city itself. This detachment of Spartans from their kin was a virtue praised but not really practiced throughout Greece.[43] Socrates's myth of the earth-born, however, has reminded us that kin-*philia* is the foundation for all *philia*, without which a city cannot exist.

The Sparta of Plato's own time had entered a serious and irreversible decline. There is increasing evidence of a drop in the number of Spartiatae over the course of the fifth century.[44] From approximately the mid-fifth century B.C.E., more and more Spartan land had fallen into the hands of fewer and fewer elite Spartans, leading to the inability of more and more poorer Spartiates to meet the required contributions to the common messes; this in turn led to the demotion of these poor Spartiates from full Spartiate status to that of "Inferiors."[45] Spartan involvement in dynastic disputes in Persia, in the politics and economics of central Greece and the Northern Aegean region, and in continuing disputes on Sicily in the twenty years after the end of the Peloponnesian War in 404 B.C.E. all contributed to a growing distrust of and hostility toward Sparta throughout Greece and the Aegean. This involvement on multiple fronts also stretched the resources of Sparta and its allies in the Peloponnesian League.[46] More and more the Spartans began to rely on manumitted helots to meet their military needs.[47] Key to Sparta's decline was the inability of the elite Spartiate class to reproduce and to maintain its domination over the lower classes. By the mid-fourth century, the number of Spartiate males had fallen to approximately one thousand, from approximately eight thousand in 480. One of the elements that led to this decline was the desire of the great landholders to keep their grip on their land and to prevent their property's being divided through dowry or inheritance; fewer offspring led to fewer demands on the property.[48] Spartan society had for centuries been based on political, religious, and economic structures that allowed the minority Spartiate elite to dominate the huge majority of the Laconian population, the *perioikoi* (free noncitizens) and the helots; those structures encouraged and institutionalized elite paranoia. With the rapid decline in the elite population, this paranoia increased. Fourth-century Sparta, then, was a city-state in decay, ruled by a rigid, dwindling elite that eventually destroyed itself.

It is with this image that Plato completes the foundation of the city. The mythic traditional subtext introduced by Socrates serves at every point to show us that this innovative city will be violent and self-destructive, and that it will, in a short time, decay into nothing. The image of Sparta with which Book 3 closes also closes the frame opened by the allusion to the Sirens: death and immobility are the results of the education that Socrates is designing. Socrates's Siren song, his untraditional myth-making, warns us to be suspicious of the story Socrates tells as he founds his city in words.

CHAPTER 4

Laws 4 and the Cyclopes

The opening discussion of the constitutions of Crete and Sparta in *Laws* 1 (624a–626b) reveals two features central to the creations of laws, constitutions, and education: they are received from a god through a human intermediary (Zeus through Minos in the case of Crete, Apollo through Lycurgus in the case of Laconia). Second, aspects of the constitution develop out of the interactions of human groups with the terrain they inhabit. The Athenian Stranger asks the Cretan, Cleinias, why does your law demand the common messes and the *gymnastikē* and weapons you employ (625c)? Cleinias replies that their *gymnastikē* has emerged from the landscape of Crete: it is not flat, so the Cretans do not use horses, but run. When running, light arms like bows and arrows are necessary. So, because of the landscape they inhabit, the Cretans have developed a particular set of military practices and a *gymnastikē* that supports that military practice. This chapter traces a part of the working-out of these two themes, the relation between terrain and political character and the role of the divine in a *politeia*, in the earlier and central books of the *Laws*. My discussion begins from the point about the relationship between constitution and terrain. I will examine the opening of Book 4, where the Stranger explains the significance for the development of virtue in the new city of the city's having a proper location and the right type of productive land; the new city's virtue will depend upon her being isolated from other cities and agriculturally self-sufficient. I will discuss this analysis in light of the Cyclopes of the *Odyssey,* another isolated and agriculturally self-sufficient group, whom the Stranger invokes in Book 3 as an example of the most just type of rule. The landscape the Cyclopes inhabit and the landscape the new city will inhabit, I will argue, indicate that the citizens of the new city will, like the Cyclopes, be characterized by hostile and closed-minded stances toward what comes to them from outside. I will turn next to a discussion of how the very opening of the *Laws* (as I have noted above) points to the crucial necessity of openness to the strange for the creation of laws and constitutions through its mention of the divine and mortal lawgivers of Crete and Sparta.

Openness to the strange reveals itself here as openness to the divine, a theme that the *Laws* pursues through the figure of Dionysus. In the final section of the chapter, I will examine what I take to be the key features of Dionysus for the *Laws:* his ability to drive humans to madness in his rites and his violent punishment of cities that refuse to be open to the divine. Plato's use of the *Odyssey* and of Dionysus myth, then, invites us to challenge some of the claims that the Stranger so authoritatively makes about the sources and nature of virtue in a city.

The Situation of the City

When concrete discussion of the construction of the new city begins in Book 4, the Stranger, following the precedent of the conversation with which the *Laws* begins, first asks Cleinias, at 704a–b, "What must one think the city is going to be? . . . I'm not asking what name it has at present or what it will be necessary to call it . . . What I mean to ask about it now is rather this: whether it will be on the sea or inland."[1] Cleinias answers that the city will be eighty stades from the sea and will have access to good harbors along the coast. Further, the land around it is highly productive, lacking in nothing (704b). There is no neighboring polis near it, because "an ancient migration from the place has left the land deserted for an incalculably long time" (704c).[2] Further, the terrain overall is rough, as is the rest of Crete, and does not provide any good stands of fir, pine, cypress, pitch pine, or plane trees, the trees used for shipbuilding (705c). The new city, then, will be inland, isolated from other cities, surrounded by land rich for agriculture but lacking ships' timber.

Since the goal of any constitution is the rearing of citizens who possess all the parts of virtue (a point developed in the early pages of Book 1, 630a and following), the Stranger's response to Cleinias's information deals with how this terrain will assist in or interfere with the developing of virtuous citizens: "it would not be incurable, at least, as regards the acquisition of virtue" (704d). He elaborates this statement as follows: the new city will be closer to the sea than it should be, but its distance from the sea will provide some protection from dangers from the sea. The dangers from the sea are primarily other people. Other people come to cities by sea and fill a city with trade and moneymaking, which give citizens untrustworthy and *palimbola* (reversible, unstable) habits (705a–b). Other people also allow citizens examples of behavior to imitate, as the Stranger indicates in his discussion of the imitating of enemies at 706a to d (I will discuss this section in more detail below). So, being some distance from the sea will protect the new city from a variety of outside influences. Further, that the land is capable of producing all the agricultural product a city could need will be good for the city, since, presumably, the city will not need to import anything from outside. That the terrain is rough, that there is not an *over*abundance of productive land, is also good, the Stranger says, as the city will not then have an excess of goods that she will export to the outside (705b).

The absence of trees used in shipbuilding is good, because it will prevent the city from easily imitating the practice of building ships and sailing around. The Stranger tells Cleinias and Megillus, the Spartan, that the people of Attica, who did not have good ship timber in their territory, did not learn the practices of shipbuilding, sailing, and naval warfare from the Cretans when Minos attacked them long ago and took the annual tribute of the seven youths and seven maidens (706b–c). At that time, they were unable to defend themselves against Minos in a sea battle with ships, which was a good thing for them, since, now that they have learned all of the practices of the sea, and, in particular, of warfare at sea, they have created among their citizens wretched habits (706d) of cowardice and changeability. The people of Attica have, in effect, become *palimboloi*, reversible. Notice the discussion of how marines behave: they attack, they run back (*palin*—the first element of the adjective *palimbolos*) to their ships, they drop their weapons and flee (706c)—they are constantly in motion, unstable, reversible.[3]

So key for the Stranger here is the isolation of the new city from the outside. Agricultural self-sufficiency will ensure that the city does not need to seek contact with other cities, other people. Absence of near neighbors will ensure that other people do not happen to come to the city by land. Distance from the sea will ensure that other people do not happen to come to the city from the sea. As the Stranger notes at 704d, virtue in the new city will depend, first of all, upon the city's isolation from all other peoples.

The laws of people in isolation have already been discussed in *Laws* Book 3, as part of the overview of the history of constitutional development. Over the course of cosmic time, the Stranger says, many thousands of cities have come into being and passed away (676b–c). The old stories tell us that disasters, such as flood and plague, have destroyed humans and left tiny groups behind (676c–677a). These tiny groups lived in the mountains, kept sheep and goats, and did not possess any of the arts of city-dwelling nor any of the vicious habits of city-dwelling (677b–679e). These people lived under the type of *politeia*, the Stranger says, that we would call a *dunasteia*, a dynasty, following *patriois nomois*, ancestral laws (680a–b). They were, in fact, the Stranger says, just like what Homer describes when he discusses the Cyclopes (680c); here the Stranger quotes *Odyssey* 9.112 to 115:

They have neither counsel-bearing assemblies, nor institutions;
rather they dwell on the peaks of lofty mountains
in hollow caves, and each one makes the law
for his children and wives, and they do not care for each other.[4]

Such people, the Stranger says a bit later, are found scattered in single houses and by tribes because of the lack of resources caused by the destructions, living under ancestral laws and living under kings (*basileuomenoi*), under a kingship that is most just (*dikaiotatēn*) (680d–e).

Note already two resonances with the material from *Laws* 4 I have just discussed: the isolation of the units and the land abandoned after a disaster (compare 4.704b–c—the site will be eighty stades from the sea and without neighbors because of "an ancient migration"). Note also the dissonance of uttering the word *dikaiotatēn* (most just) in a context describing the practices of the Cyclopes, whom the Stranger explicitly identifies at 680c. The text does not merely rely on our recognizing the precise context of the quote but makes a point of *naming* the Cyclopes, renowned, because of the *Odyssey*'s Polyphemus, as examples of idiosyncrasy and violence, two qualities quite opposed, in Greek eyes, to the possession of *dikē*.[5] So this quote and the claim that this kind of regime is the most just kingship stand as a problem demanding more scrutiny and more thinking.

The Cyclopes

To understand what the text could be asking us to think about here, I turn to the section of the *Odyssey* that the Stranger quotes. These lines are part of Odysseus's description of the land of the Cyclopes as he relates his wanderings before the court of Alcinous, king of the Phaeacians (*Odyssey* 9.106–41). The lines that the Stranger quotes appear close to the beginning of this passage. What I want to establish here is that the terrain of the land of the Cyclopes and the terrain of new city have two important characteristics in common. Given that Book 1 and the Stranger's discussion of terrain in Book 4 have told us that terrain determines constitution, which determines the character of the citizens, it should be the case that similar terrains lead to similar characters.

First of all, in 9.107–11, the poem tells us that the Cyclopes, outrageous and lawless (*huperphialōn athemistōn*, line 106):

> . . . trusting in the immortal gods
> neither plant a plant with their hands nor plow,

> but everything grows unsown and unplowed,
> wheat and barley and grape vines, which also bear   110
> wine rich in grapes, and Zeus's rain makes it grow for them.

This land, like the land of the new city, is lacking in nothing in terms of agricultural produce, although here, of course, there is no agriculture, as the earth produces without the Cyclopes needing to cultivate it. The Cyclopes and the new city are both self-sufficient (compare *Laws* 4.704b). The Cyclopes, further, are isolated. Their isolation depends not simply on their being in that part of the world that is off the map, the part of the world in which Odysseus's wanderings take place, but on their not having the ability to use the sea to travel. They live across a stretch of sea from an island that is perfect for habitation: it possesses forest, goats, arable land, meadows, and a good harbor (*Odyssey* 9.116–39). The Cyclopes do not come to this island because (*Odyssey* 9.125–30) they do not have ships or shipbuilders; if they had they could sail "to each city of human beings as men do, crossing the sea with their ships to each other." The Cyclopes are kept to one place because they cannot leave it. The Stranger hopes that the citizens in the new city, in the same way, will not be able to leave the city because they, like the Cyclopes, will not have ships. Ships, in the *Odyssey* passage, are explicitly linked with two things: contact with cities and other peoples and the foundation of new settlements. (The Cyclopes, if they could sail to the habitable island, could make it a "well-founded" dwelling, *Odyssey* 9.130.) Contact with other humans is precisely the thing that the Stranger wants the new city to avoid. In both the *Odyssey* and the *Laws,* then, we see the same themes, self-sufficiency and isolation, emerge.[6]

What, then, are the Cyclopes like, and how can their practices be said to be related to the terrain in which they dwell? Our understanding of the Cyclopes depends largely upon the behavior of Polyphemus, visited by Odysseus and twelve of his companions. Polyphemus kills some of Odysseus's companions and eats them raw, trapping those left alive inside his cave with a great boulder. In Polyphemus's behavior we see the greatest example of the violation of the practices of hospitality that the *Odyssey* offers. Polyphemus himself does not explain his behavior, except insofar as he says, when Odysseus beseeches him for a guest-gift and appropriate hospitality in the name of Zeus, protector of strangers (*Odyssey* 9.266–71), that the Cyclopes, being better than the gods, do not worry about Zeus; Poylphemus says he would not spare Odysseus simply out of fear of retribution from Zeus if he felt like doing him harm (*Odyssey* 9.273–79). So the Cyclopes are not bound by the same divine laws, the laws of *xenia*, hospitality, that bind human beings.

That freedom does not explain *why* Polyphemus acts as he does, though. It explains *how* he can act as he does without fear of the gods.

In part, I think, we see why Polyphemus eats Odysseus's companions in the opening description of the land of the Cyclopes at *Odyssey* 8.106–41. In this land, the earth produces for the Cyclopes everything that they need out of the soil, grains, and grapes; for other needs they herd goats and sheep. The Cyclopes are beings in whose world everything that appears is *for their use.* Earth produces, they eat what it produces. Animals are there, they eat the animals. Their only experience of life that is not Cyclopean life is that it is to be exploited and destroyed. When, returning from a day spent herding his flock, Polyphemus finds Odysseus and his companions waiting in his cave, what he finds is another version of earth producing for him from itself. He knows that Odysseus and his companions must have come to his land from across the sea and asks them why they have come here (*Odyssey* 9.252–55), but displays no particular interest in Odysseus's reply, other than to say that he will treat the strangers as he sees fit. Then he kills and eats two of the companions (*Odyssey* 9.287–93). The strangers are present and vulnerable or open to him, just as a sheep is vulnerable or open to him, or a grapevine, and he treats them as he would treat other life that comes beneath his hand: he eats them. The land that produces in itself all of our needs leads us to regard everything that appears before us as for *our* needs. The world exists *for us,* not for others, not for itself.[7]

It is precisely this stance toward others that Cyclopean isolation encourages. Not having access to the rest of the world means not having access to, as the poem tells us, the cities of human beings (*Odyssey* 9.128).[8] The proem of the *Odyssey* tells us that it will sing the man of many ways who wandered much and saw the cities and knew the minds of many men (*Odyssey* 1.1–3); the wanderings themselves, as Odysseus narrates them in the central books of the poem, insist on his travels forcing him to develop a new understanding of how he sees his own relationship to strangers. We see a progression from the marauding pirate as whom he begins his wanderings, as he and his companions fall upon and sack the city of the Cicones, killing the people and taking their wives and possessions as spoil (*Odyssey* 9.39–42)[9] to the assimilable gracious guest of Alcinous and the Phaeacians. Contact with strangers, with the cities and minds of others, has forced Odysseus to cease to regard the world as *for him.*[10]

The self-sufficiency and isolation of the Cyclopes, then, lead them to destroy what comes to them by eating it. This is their habit, their not-quite-immediate response to what is not themselves. In the same way, when we turn back to Book 4 of the *Laws,* we see a similar habit developing: what comes from outside, what is not us, can only be harmful to us. The Stranger argues that the city's isolation is what will ensure its virtue because the influence of outsiders through trade and warfare will only be harmful to the city. We in the new city, rather than seeing the world as *for us*, will see it as *not* for us. In either case, we do not let what comes from outside tell us what it is. We already know.

So, in light of the invocation of the Cyclopes in Book 3, we see that the new city's terrain already indicates that she will foster citizens who are not *open* to the strange, insofar as they will know what the strange, the *xenos*, is before they meet it. The strange is what we must reject and fear. The discussion in Book 4 does not regard this prejudice as problematic; indeed, it will serve as the motivation for many of the laws concerning education, trade, and the like, that the Stranger goes on to articulate. It is nonetheless the case that the *Laws* itself has already indicated at least one way in which openness to the strange is critical to a city and her laws: laws, constitutions, are not things that human beings simply make up themselves. Rather, laws come to us from the gods and come to us through human intermediaries. The opening of the dialogue, as I noted at the beginning of my discussion, reminds us that the Cretans received their laws from Zeus through Minos and the Spartans received their laws from Apollo through Lycurgus.[11] To the first humans to receive these constitutions, they must have seemed a radical change from current ways of thinking and acting.[12] For these divine utterances to become constitutions, laws, for human beings, the people of Crete and Laconia must have been *open* to accepting them. The new, the strange, coming from outside, from a god, had to be something they could accept.

Keeping these things in mind, when we turn again to the new city in Book 4 we see that the Stranger argues as follows: at 709a–c he says that god, chance, opportunity, and art guide all human affairs; human beings themselves are not simply self-directing, but depend on these other forces, especially for the framing of laws. The good lawgiver, faced with installing his laws in a city, would ask to have a city governed by a tyrant (*turannoumenēn polin*) (709c). Under a tyrant, he says (710b), the lawgiver's laws would be accepted most quickly and easily. At 711b–c, the Stranger notes that the tyrant, of all rulers, can most effectively serve as an example to the people of his city, so that he may turn them toward virtue through praise if they follow his example and through dishonor if they do not. Cleinias wonders at this point why citizens will follow the tyrant, who will be using a combination of persuasion and violence (*peithō* and *bia*) (711c). The Stranger replies that no one could ever change a constitution more quickly than an all-powerful ruler (711c). So in *one* specific instance—tyranny—the openness of citizens to change is not important. The tyrant will change things as he sees fit using whatever method he chooses, persuasion or violence. He can impose his will. In any other type of city, then, it must be the case that citizen openness to transformation of the laws is necessary and crucial.

Further, the Stranger has argued in Book 3 that the lawgiver must aim at three things: that the city be free, that the city be a friend (*philē*) to itself, and that the city have intelligence (*nous*) (701d). The laws should, then, create a city that, among other things, participates in the hallmark of the divine, reason and understanding.[13] The gods, then, in the stories of Minos and Lycurgus, and in the very notion of law itself, are the sources of law for humans. We receive divine law through other human beings, lawgivers, and so we must be prepared to accept, to be open to, the divine as it comes to us through humans. We can recall Polyphemus, who marks himself as lawless, particularly concerning hospitality, when he tells Odysseus that he has no fear of Zeus and the other gods and so will not restrain himself in any way out of respect for the gods' laws. If we are not to be like Polyphemus, we must, in the end, be open to the divine.[14]

This point about the necessity of openness to the divine as the provider of law is not merely implicit in these stories of Minos, Zeus, Apollo, and Lycurgus, nor in the account of the ease with which a tyrant can install the constitution of the lawgiver; openness to the divine is a thread that runs throughout the *Laws*. It is at play perhaps most clearly in the use the dialogue makes of Dionysus, and so it is to Dionysus I now turn.

Dionysus

The god first appears in Book 1, at 637 b–c, in a reference to one of his festivals, the Dionysia. Megillus the Spartan complains that people (not Spartans, of course) use the festival as an excuse to yield to all sorts of pleasures once they get drunk; he has seen this behavior at Athens and at Taras, Sparta's colony in Italy. The Stranger's response here is interesting: he notes that any stranger amazed at (*thaumazōn*) what he is not used to at home should be reminded that this is how law is *here* and that maybe the law is different in his home (637c). There are two things initially worthy of note here: what causes amazement, *thauma*, is strangeness, lack of familiarity, and the response to *thauma*, as evinced by Megillus, can be to condemn what is not familiar and what is not understood.[15] The *proper* response, articulated by the Stranger, is to see that the unfamiliar can be law, *nomos*, that it has its own meaning, history, and place.[16] In the example here, the Dionysia at Athens and Taras, we see that the rituals of a place, the way one city honors a god recognized and shared by all Greek cities, can cause amazement to a stranger.[17] He can be not open to the divine as it manifests itself outside his own home. Second I note that this expression of open-mindedness comes in a context involving Dionysus.

We next meet Dionysus in Book 2, in the discussion of the importance of holidays and festivities that opens the book. Holidays are necessary, the Stranger says, to help us resuscitate what we learned over the course of our education about good attitudes toward pain and pleasure (653c). The gods give us periods of rest from work, and they have given us the Muses, Apollo, and Dionysus as the gods who will, as fellow celebrators (*suneortastai*), set us back upright again (653d). The gods mentioned here are of course the gods in charge of musical performance. What is being invoked especially is choral performance. Dionysus oversees choral performance as the god of group identity; the Muses as performers are always a chorus; Apollo is here called *mousēgetēs*, leader of the Muses, indicating that he is chorus leader of the Muses, a typical performance role for him.[18] It is choral music that is discussed over the course of Book 2. The Stranger also refers to these gods as fellow celebrators, *suneortastai,* implying that these gods are present to us when we celebrate. This implication is odd for Apollo and the Muses: on the traditional Greek understanding, we do not meet these gods face-to-face in our world.[19] For Dionysus it is commonplace, as he alone among the gods is conceived as present with his worshipers at their festivities; he is one of the celebrating group.[20] The Stranger installs Dionysus here as crucial to education and crucial to the maintenance of the lessons of education in later life. His chorus of elders in the revised drinking curriculum of Books 1 and 2 will serve as models for appropriate singing and as singers of the best and most beautiful things (665 a–d).

Toward the end of Book 2, another aspect of Dionysus is raised: his role as the god of *mania*, madness (672a–c). Drunkenness is a variety of madness that, the Stranger says, people misinterpret and condemn when they should not.[21] He tells a story, an etiological tale about the origins of *mania* among humans, which he also says we should perhaps not tell (672b). The story goes as follows: Dionysus's sense was struck out of his soul by Hera; as vengeance the god inflicted Bacchic *mania* along with choruses and wine on human beings. *Mania* is what causes sensible things to cry out and jump about randomly when they are young. This crying out and jumping are what give rise to *mousikē* and *gymnastikē* and are also what allow us to perceive rhythm and harmony (672d). *Mania*, then, produces the two central planks of education. So *mania* in this basic but important way is not something to condemn.

The story the Stranger tells here is significant: Hera made Dionysus lose his senses, and so he installed important aspects of his own worship among human beings. We seem to have here an allusion to and an adaptation of the most common type of myth of Dionysus, in which the god is not recognized and so punishes people (the "recognition myth"). The association of Hera, madness, and Dionysus seems to point to a particular myth, the myth of Lycurgus.[22] The best-known version of this myth appears at *Iliad* 6.130–40. The common features of the various versions are roughly as follows: Hera instigates Lycurgus to attack Dionysus, who is mad and on earth with a group of women. Dionysus flees before his attacker. Lycurgus is punished in a variety of ways, none of which involves the installation of rituals.[23] The Lycurgus myth, in its extant formulations, does *not* follow the pattern of the recognition myth, which includes, as *its* concluding moment, the installation-of-ritual function. Euripides's *Bacchae* provides the most thorough working-out of the Dionysiac recognition-myth pattern, which contains the following five elements:

> 1. Dionysus appears *in disguise* among humans to ask for recognition of his rites.
> 2. The group or representatives of the group refuse to acknowledge the god; they resist the new and innovative relationship with the divine that he offers.
> 3. The god drives the offenders mad and forces them out into the wild.
> 4. The god has humans destroy children within their own household.
> 5. The god, now recognized, installs his rites within the group of humans.[24]

The Stranger's story of the introduction of *mania* to humans by Dionysus, then, takes one fairly common myth, the myth of Dionysus and Lycurgus, and adds a final element, the institution of a ritual, from the dominant Dionysus myth-type. This invocation of the recognition myth reminds us of the violence of the god's anger at humans who refuse to be open to the strange.

Dionysus is the god of the mask, the *xenos,* and the stranger par excellence. Dionysus is the god who reminds us always of the crucial importance of not rejecting the one who comes to us from outside and who, as he does in the *Bacchae,* upsets us.[25] He overturns the customary order of the city, driving women out of their homes, out of the city, to dance in the wild places. He intoxicates, he unifies, and he terrifies. He is not moderate, and he demands that we not be moderate, too. The recognition myth insists on the god's hostility to the staid order of the city-state, manifested in part through his driving us to dance. Book 7 of the *Laws* alludes to Dionysus's relation to the city-state when it discusses the dances of Dionysus. The Stranger enumerates types of dance: warlike dance, like the Pyrrhic dance that imitates combat (815a), and peaceful dance in honor of the gods (815d–e). These are dances of a *politikon genos,* a political type, unlike *Bacchic* dancing, in which drunken people imitate ritual and members of the Dionysiac retinue, like satyrs (815c). This dance is not warlike, not peaceful, not *politikon.* Like the god in whose honor it is performed, Bacchic dance is not *of* the city.

Dionysus is the god who manifests himself as hostile to city order, as *not politikos;* yet he is a crucial god for every Greek city-state, as he is for the new city. His function in the city is to refresh, to allow us to turn from the everyday world of work to festivity and to madness. His madness allows us to see the new, to jump, to dance. His madness also comes in a more violent form as punishment—punishment in which we humans are the agents—when we refuse to be open, when we take up the Stranger only as dangerous, only as abusable because of his danger. Dionysus is the god who tells us not to manifest the Spartan Megillus's response to *thauma* at the unfamiliar, rejection and condemnation. Dionysus is, further, the god who, as the one who drives us out of our households and out of the city, overcomes the tendency of humans within cities toward introversion and isolation.[26] He is the god who enforces our openness to each other, to other households, to other cities, and to the new; he ensures that we not isolate ourselves in our comfortable, familiar, homely understanding of the world. He is the god whose task in all Greek city-states is to fight against the very isolation and closed-mindedness that the Stranger insists will be the strength of the new city.

Openness and Tradition

The two planks of law-creation in *Laws* 1, then, that laws be received from a god and that laws emerge from humans' relationships with their landscape, tell us that, in our relationship with our laws, we humans must, as political groups, be open to the strange and the new. That is, we cannot be like the Cyclopes of the *Odyssey,* taking up everything that comes to us in exactly the same way because we refuse to acknowledge that the strange can have anything to say to us to which we must attend. This Cyclopean stance of closed-mindedness derives from the landscape the Cyclopes inhabit; as does the fact that they are, as a society, static. They have no political organization, and they are technologically retarded. Their self-sufficiency, isolation, and closed-mindedness also ensure that they will never change—they will not on their own discover anything new, and they will never receive and accept anything new from outside.

The discussion in *Laws* 4 of the terrain and situation for the new city-foundation portrays this location as remarkably similar to the situation of the Odyssean Cyclopes. The Stranger insists that isolation and agricultural self-sufficiency, far from being a problem, will ensure that the new foundation will be a virtuous and successful city-state. Despite his assertions, though, our knowledge of the Cyclopes tells us that isolation and rejection of the strange can result in internal stagnation and violent hostility to the external.[27] The traditional material, the *Odyssey*'s Cyclopes, invoked by the Stranger himself in Book 3, and the authoritative layer-down of laws, the Athenian Stranger, are not telling the same story.

The possibility that the Stranger's story is not necessarily one we should accept is strengthened by the terms in which the dialogue invokes and describes the god Dionysus. When Megillus complains in Book 1 that people outside Sparta use the god's festivals as justification for self-indulgence, the Stranger tells Megillus that he should not dismiss and condemn what is not familiar to him; Dionysus is the figure around whom the notion of political open-mindedness crystallizes. In Book 2, the Stranger sets Dionysus up as one of the gods central to the new city, alluding to the common Dionysiac "recognition myth," in which the god descends upon cities that reject the new and the strange, punishes them, and purifies them by instituting his own worship. Dionysus—a god crucial to the ancient Greek city-state through his associations with political openness and his hostility to seclusion and introversion within the city-state—is precisely opposed to the very things that the Stranger claims will be the securers of virtue and success in the new foundation: isolation and self-sufficiency.

When the Stranger appeals to and uses traditional material, the Odyssean Cyclopes and the myths and associations of Dionysus, then, he opens up systems of meaning and knowledge that consistently run counter to the claims he explicitly makes. The Cyclopes remind us that isolated and self-sufficient societies can be static, closed-minded, and hostile to what is new and what is coming from the outside. They suggest to us that the proposals for lawmaking that insist on isolation for the new city could well result in an unhealthy political failure. Dionysus reminds us that we all know that openness to the new and the strange is critically important for the maintenance of a healthy, productive city-state. Through his deployment of this traditional material, then, Plato offers us, his readers, an avenue through which to challenge the monologic authority of the Stranger. Plato invites us to participate in the conversation that his text portrays. Indeed, Plato portrays the tradition itself as part of the conversation, not as explicit participant, but as an underlying and informing system of thought, meaning, and understanding that allows us not to take words at their face value, but to be open to what is present but not explicit in his text.[28]

PART III

Philosophy and Tradition

CHAPTER 5

The *Apology* and Oedipus

When considering Plato's attitude toward myth, we must be clear about what we mean when we say "myth" in a Platonic context. As I noted in chapter 3, when I refer to "myth," I mean "a traditional tale used by a culture to tell itself something important about itself." By "traditional" I mean "accepted by being told and retold over time."[1] By that definition, the things we often refer to as "myths" in Plato, such as the Myth of Er in *Republic* 10 or the Great Myth of the *Phaedrus,* really are not myths. They are *muthoi*—stories. When Plato talks about myth, as I said above, he speaks of "what the poets say"—that is, narrative performance poems about the traditional tales. When Plato refers to what the poets say, he generally has Socrates say damning things about it. For example, at *Republic* 377d–e, as we saw in chapter 3, Socrates says that Homer, Hesiod, and the other poets tell lies about the gods, so we have to condemn them. At *Republic* 600e–601b, Socrates says that poets are imitators of images of excellence who have no understanding of what they say; consequently there is no good in what they say. At *Apology* 22a–c, Socrates describes his experience examining the poets: they say many fine things in their poems but know nothing of what they say. Because what the poets say can be false and because poets never understand what they are talking about, proper education has to be careful about how it uses poetry. The traditional stories can set a bad example for the young (*Republic* 391e), and performing the traditional stories can lead to the development of bad habits (*Republic* 395c). Despite the fact that Socrates says all these condemnatory things about what the poets say, over and over again we see him *using* the poets. He quotes them, he holds them up as authorities, and he explicates them. As we have already seen in earlier chapters on the *Republic* and the *Laws*, Plato, too, uses myth in a subtle and allusive way, and I will argue in this chapter that this practice is also powerfully at play in the *Apology*.

Through looking carefully at the terms in which Socrates narrates his autobiography in the *Apology,* we will see that Plato uses the story of Oedipus as the background of Socrates's life story. Recognizing this traditional mythic background will help us better understand the role of philosophy in Socrates's life, and the revolutionary way that Socratic philosophy transforms traditional norms. I will begin by retelling the story of Oedipus as we find it in Sophocles's tragedies *Oedipus Tyrannus* and *Oedipus at Colonus*. I will focus on Oedipus's setting out to do an *elenchos*—a test or refutation—of the oracle of Apollo by engaging in an investigation, a *zētēsis*. Next I will look at Socrates's account of his own attempt to do an *elenchos* of the oracle by doing a *zētēsis*. Socrates, we shall see, is a mirror of Oedipus. By invoking the terms of Oedipus, Plato effectively establishes a mythic sanction for the person and the method of Socrates. At the same time, there is a crucial difference between Socrates and Oedipus, in that Socrates is a figure of self-knowledge. Plato's figuring of Socrates as Oedipus, then, also functions to transform the significance of the traditional mythic terms. This theme of self-knowledge will lead further to a comparison of Socrates with the figure of Teiresias, by which we will see that Socrates and Plato lay claim to a right to philosophy that exceeds the limited terms of Athenian culture and law. I will conclude by arguing that, through his presentation of Socrates, Plato presents philosophy and tradition as in reciprocal relation with each other, philosophical self-knowledge depending upon tradition to supply it with the terms of possible meaning, and tradition depending upon philosophy to supply it with the self-conscious engagement with living reality that makes tradition actually meaningful.

Oedipus

The story of Oedipus is a familiar one and appeared in many different versions in ancient Greece. Best known to us nowadays is of course Sophocles's version of Oedipus in his tragedies *Oedipus Tyrannus* and *Oedipus at Colonus*. This Sophoclean version is also the one that is pertinent for our discussion of the *Apology*. I shall begin by retelling this traditional tale as Sophocles tells it.

The king and queen of Thebes, Laius and Jocasta, receive an oracle from Apollo that tells them that Laius will be killed by his son by Jocasta. Consequently, when a son is born to them, they send the infant to be exposed on Mount Cithaeron near Thebes. The servant entrusted with this task does not expose the child, however, but gives him instead to a shepherd from Corinth, who takes the boy and gives him to the king and queen of Corinth, Polybus and Merope. These two raise the child as their own and name him Oedipus, *Swollen-foot*, because of the infection in his mutilated feet. When Oedipus is a young man, a drunken man at a banquet tells him that he is a bastard.

Angry, Oedipus asks Polybus and Merope to explain, but they deny the story. Later Oedipus goes to the oracle of Apollo at Delphi to consult the god about his true parentage.

The god does not tell Oedipus who his parents are; instead he tells Oedipus that he will kill his father and have children by his mother. Oedipus, determined to ensure that the prophecy not come true and believing still that Polybus and Merope are his parents, resolves never to return to Corinth. So he sets off to wander. He comes to a place where three roads meet and is confronted by an old man in a carriage accompanied by a sizable retinue of attendants. The old man and his attendants try to push Oedipus out of the road. Angry, Oedipus kills the old man and almost all of the attendants and continues down the road. This old man, whose identity Oedipus never learns, is Laius of Thebes. The road eventually brings Oedipus to Thebes where, by solving a riddle, he destroys the monstrous Sphinx that is plaguing the city. As a reward for his service, he is given the recently widowed queen, Jocasta, as his wife. He and Jocasta reign peacefully for many years and have four children together: Polyneices, Eteocles, Antigone, and Ismene. Oedipus has unwittingly fulfilled Apollo's prophecy.

After many years, a plague falls on Thebes. To learn how to deal with this plague, Oedipus sends Jocasta's brother Creon to Delphi to consult Apollo. Creon returns to say that the plague is punishment for the fact that the Thebans have never found and punished the murderer of the previous king, Laius. Oedipus vows that he will find the killer and either kill him or send him into exile. He decides to do an investigation—a *zētēsis* (*Oedipus Tyrannus* 110, 266, 362, 450). To discover the murderer after so many years, Oedipus summons the blind seer Teiresias to ask him what he knows. Teiresias, who of course knows the truth, refuses to tell Oedipus anything. Angry, Oedipus accuses Teiresias of plotting against him; in response Teiresias tells Oedipus that he is the killer and that he does not know the truth of his own identity. Oedipus grows even angrier and decides that Creon must be involved in this plot to discredit him. He accuses Creon of fabricating the oracle. Creon tells Oedipus to test his report—to do an *elenchos* (*Oedipus Tyrannus* 603–10). Eventually, through his investigation, which involves questioning Creon, Jocasta, Teiresias, and finally the servant who was responsible for exposing the infant Oedipus on Mount Cithaeron, Oedipus learns that he is the killer of Laius, that Laius and Jocasta are his parents, and that he has fulfilled the prophecy that he spent his life resisting. Jocasta kills herself when she realizes the truth. Oedipus blinds himself with her dress-pins and demands that Creon send him into exile. Creon refuses to act in this matter without taking advice, so the play closes with the fate of Oedipus undecided.

The *Oedipus at Colonus* is set years after the blinding of Oedipus. Oedipus's two sons took over rule of Thebes when they were old enough; at that time they decided to expel their father from Thebes. Oedipus and his daughter Antigone wandered Greece seeking refuge and being denied rest because of Oedipus's pollution of kin-murder and incest. Eventually they come to a deme of Athens, Colonus, where there is a precinct of the Furies. Apollo has told Oedipus to come to this place; he has told him, further, that this will be the site of his death and that the place where his bones lie will profit from their presence. Oedipus appeals to Theseus, the king of Athens, for sanctuary and informs him of the god's promise that Oedipus will bring good things to the city that takes him in. Theseus grants Oedipus sanctuary and then has to protect Oedipus and his daughters from Creon and Polyneices, each of whom has come to Athens in search of Oedipus, having learned of the blessings that Oedipus will bring. Oedipus gets angry at both Creon and Polyneices. He then goes off into the grove of the Furies with Theseus and dies mysteriously. Only Theseus and the subsequent kings of Athens will ever know the precise location of Oedipus's grave.

There are two main points that I want to take away from this story: first, Oedipus's early life is devoted to ensuring that the oracle about him never comes true. He wants, in essence, to refute the god. His investigation into the death of Laius again is an attempt to refute what two people—Teiresias and Creon—have told him Apollo said. The second half of *Oedipus Tyrannus* is thus devoted to Oedipus's *elenchos* of Apollo's words. Apollo is, of course, proved right. Second, Oedipus is driven out of Thebes and wanders to Athens (he describes himself as *planētēn Oidipoun*, the wandering Oedipus, at *Oedipus at Colonus* 3). His suffering transforms him from a pollution to a benefit. Oedipus is good for Athens: he is a profit—*kerdos* (*Oedipus at Colonus* 84, 576–78); he brings benefit—*onēsis* (287–88); he is a savior—*sōtēr* (463); he brings power—*kratos* (1331–32); his presence is a gift—*dōsōn* (576), *dōrēma* (647).[2]

Socrates

The *Apology* gives us Socrates's account of his own life. One of the charges against him is impiety, introducing new gods. Although Socrates never comes right out and says so, his account of why he has pursued the life that has gotten him into so much trouble (questioning people) is a demonstration that this charge is untrue. Socrates's whole life has been a service to Apollo. In this section, I will work through Socrates's autobiography, pointing out the ways in which this life is also the life of Oedipus.

Socrates starts his life of questioning because of an oracle of Apollo. Socrates's friend Chairephon went to Delphi and asked if someone was wiser than Socrates. The priestess of Apollo replied that no one was wiser than Socrates (21a). Socrates was puzzled by this response, since, he says, he was not aware of being wise at all (21b). So after a long time Socrates decided to *investigate* the god, to do a *zētēsis* (21b). His goal was simply to find someone wiser than himself and to prove thereby that the god was wrong: he wanted to do an *elenchos* of the god's utterance—*elenxōn to manteion* (21c).[3]

Compare Socrates and Oedipus here. Both receive oracles via a third party (Chairephon and Creon). Both cannot accept what they are told. Both set out on an investigation with the goal of doing a test. The investigation involves asking other people questions. The similarity does not consist just in the actions that the two perform; both *Oedipus Tyrannus* and the *Apology* use the same words to describe what Oedipus and Socrates are doing: *zētēsis* and *elenchos*. The *Apology* thus sets Socrates up as a mirror of Sophocles's Oedipus; the similarity manifests itself in a basic narrative identity and in Plato's use of Sophoclean diction to describe his Socrates.[4] Let us consider further aspects of the investigations of Oedipus and Socrates.

Oedipus commences an investigation with a particular goal: to discover the murderer of Laius. Oedipus begins his investigation with a firm conviction: that he himself is not Laius's killer. Oedipus discovers that *he* killed Laius (and in the process learns that Laius and Jocasta are his parents). Oedipus completes his investigation having learned things that are, to say the least, not what he had expected to learn: Oedipus discovers a truth that challenges the commonly held belief in Thebes that Laius and all his attendants were killed by a band of robbers, not by one man alone. More significantly, Oedipus discovers that he himself is not who he thought he was. Similarly, Socrates's *zētēsis* begins from a firm conviction—his belief that the oracle is wrong because he, Socrates, is not wise—and the pursuit of the investigation involves a transformation in which commonly held beliefs are found to be mistaken and he is led to change his interpretation of his own wisdom. The end of the investigation for both—an investigation prompted by the oracle from Apollo—is not what either envisions when he begins. Let us consider the particular transformations that Socrates goes through in his investigation.

To refute the oracle and to find someone wiser than himself, Socrates initiated many encounters with people commonly reputed to be wise and, he tells us, the same thing happened over and over, namely, those he questioned revealed themselves not to know what they thought they knew. He persisted in this investigation because, he says, he had to take the matter of the god seriously (21e). Socrates's first goal was to prove the god wrong, and this goal arose out of his own discomfort with the oracle. But this remark at 21e makes clear that, early on, Socrates recognized that this investigation was not simply his own gratuitous decision, not simply a matter of attending to his own comfort or discomfort, but something necessary and something that involved the god. Socrates's attitude shifts from doing something for himself to taking the matter of the god seriously, and in his further references to the motives for his investigation we see that his attitude comes to change even more: his diction shifts to indicating that, far from doing this for himself, he is doing his investigation *for Apollo.* At 22a4 Socrates says, "As I was doing my investigation at the god's request (*kata ton theon*), I discovered that the people with the biggest reputations were the biggest fools."[5] He speaks of investigating the poets next, then the craftsmen. When he sees that the craftsmen at least knew their crafts, but they also made the mistake of thinking they knew other things when they did not (22d), he asks himself "on behalf of the oracle (*huper tou chrēsmou*)" if he would like to be like the craftsmen or like himself (22e). He replies to himself and to the oracle (*tōi chrēsmōi*) that he is better off as he is (22e). Socrates thus comes to interpret his quest as one undertaken *on behalf of* Apollo and his oracle. At the end of this investigation, Socrates, having been unable to find anyone wiser than himself, has made many enemies and has gotten a reputation as wise (22e–23a), but that view of himself, Socrates says, is wrong. Now *defending* the oracle, Socrates says that in truth the god is wise and the oracle that no one is wiser than Socrates probably means that human wisdom is without value (23a).

Having set out to refute the oracle, then, Socrates has, because of what he has learned, become an *interpreter* of Apollo. Socrates goes on at 23b to speak for Apollo and say that the oracle means that a man is wise who, like Socrates, knows that he is worth nothing with respect to wisdom. Socrates has discovered that he *cannot* prove the oracle wrong. He has in fact vindicated the god. He has given his life up to vindicating the god and to trying to understand what the god initially meant. His whole investigation proceeded from the view that "no one is wiser than Socrates" meant "Socrates is wise." That had to be wrong, since Socrates knew he *was not* wise. Socrates learned what "being wise" means as he tried to find someone wiser than himself.

Thus Socrates, like Oedipus, *learns* what the oracle means, after wrongly thinking its meaning to be obvious. This is itself a familiar scenario: Apollo's oracles are notoriously obscure, and people are always misinterpreting them. In his *Histories,* for example, Herodotus tells the story of how Croesus of Lydia consulted the oracle at Delphi about whether or not to declare war against King Cyrus of Persia. The god replied that if Croesus attacked Cyrus he would destroy a great kingdom. Croesus took this response to mean that he would be victorious against Cyrus, attacked the Persians, and lost his own kingdom.[6] This and the story of Oedipus are the best-known examples of misunderstanding of oracles from Delphi, and they are typical: the person consulting the god receives the oracle, misunderstands it, acts on the misunderstanding, and discovers through these misguided actions what the correct interpretation of the oracle in fact is. In this way, Socrates's story in the *Apology* follows the familiar pattern: he takes the oracle to mean one thing, acts on that interpretation, and discovers in the course of the investigation he undertakes that the oracle means something else. Oedipus and Socrates share a distinctive feature, though, that is *not* typical of the misunderstood oracle theme: their misinterpretations of the oracles result in their attempts to *resist* the god. It is distinctive that both resist the oracle and are compelled to realize their mistake. Further, as a result of their misunderstandings, both of them end up devoted to the word of Apollo, thereby doing good to Athens.

Oedipus and Socrates both come to recognize that the god is inescapable. Oedipus, specifically, leaves Thebes and trusts Apollo to guide him to his final resting place in Athens in *Oedipus at Colonus*. This wandering is another aspect that Oedipus and Socrates seem to have in common. Socrates devotes his life to seeking and not finding wisdom and then trying to reveal to people their folly, and at *Apology* 22a Socrates describes this by making what is generally taken to be an allusion to the wanderings of Odysseus and to the twelve labors of Heracles; he says, "I must display for you my wandering (*planēn*) as I was, as it were, laboring some labors (*ponous tinas ponountos*)." While I certainly do not want to maintain that this passage is not in fact an allusion to these two heroes, I suggest that, given the parallels to Oedipus set up in the rest of Socrates's account of his quest, we also see here a continuing allusion to Sophocles's Oedipus.[7] As I have already noted, Oedipus and Antigone wander Greece for many years before they arrive in Athens, and Oedipus opens the play by referring to himself as the *planētēs* Oedipus. The word I have translated as "labor" above, *ponos*, does not mean just hard work or toil, but suffering, distress. This word and its verb, *poneō*, appear in *Oedipus at Colonus* twelve times.[8] Both wandering and *ponos* are distinctly marked out as belonging both to Sophocles's Oedipus and to Plato's Socrates.

The final result of these divinely inspired wanderings points to a further parallel between Oedipus and Socrates. According to *Oedipus at Colonus*, Oedipus, having completed his wanderings, dies near Athens, and his grave becomes part of civic cult: he becomes a tutelary or "protecting" hero. This transformation, indeed, is not simply the stuff of Sophocles's drama: it is historical fact. Among their *polis* heroes, the Athenians included Oedipus, pointing to his tomb in the precinct of the Furies near the Areopagus in the deme Colonus.[9] In this hero cult, Oedipus's characteristic anger is directed against the enemies of Athens and thereby protects the city. Oedipus is thus ultimately a benefit to, and protector of, Athens. In the *Apology,* similarly, Socrates presents himself as serving a beneficial and protective function for Athens. At 29e–30a, Socrates tells the assembly that his questioning and testing of the citizens of Athens are undertaken at the command of the god (*keleuei ho theos*) and that no greater good has ever come to be in the city than his service to the god. Oedipus is a "gift" of Apollo to Athens (*Oedipus at Colonus* 576, 647), and, at 30d, Socrates refers to himself and his questioning as a gift (*dosis*) from the god to the Athenians.[10] The particular form that Socrates's benefits to Athens take is his attempt to help her citizens toward the truth he has come to: he tries to persuade people to care about becoming good and thoughtful and about having Athens be a good and thoughtful city (36c). Socrates also identifies himself as protecting the citizens of Athens: after the decision to execute him is taken, Socrates prophesies that after this death there will be no one to restrain the young men from questioning and rebuking those who have voted to put Socrates to death far more harshly than Socrates ever did (39c–d). Both Oedipus and Socrates, having undergone the overturning of their original interpretations of Apollo's oracle, are transformed into the same thing: devotees of Apollo who serve and protect Athens.

One final comparison points ultimately to an important difference that is highlighted by the comparison of Oedipus and Socrates. Socrates, famously, never does find anyone wiser than himself. Over and over again, Socrates finds out that the people he talks to and questions "think they know something, but do not." Socrates comes to see that he is different from all of these others only in that he knows that he does not know anything (e.g. 21c–e). Socrates thus apparently knows something that no one else knows: in knowing that he does not know, he knows something about *himself.* It is this knowledge that, he concludes, constitutes whatever wisdom he has. In this particular way, then, wisdom for Socrates involves knowing something.[11] Let us compare Oedipus, who also has a distinctive knowledge that others lack.

Most prominently, Oedipus is the one whose intellect solves the riddle of the Sphinx (*Oedipus Tyrannus* 35–38, 391–98). Traditionally, Oedipus is said to have recognized that "what walks on four legs in the morning, two legs in the afternoon, and three legs at night" is "a man." Oedipus saved Thebes from the plague of the Sphinx by being able to recognize human nature—specifically, being able to recognize the characteristic pattern of human bodily life. Oedipus is also a figure of unique knowledge in that he is the one who, through his investigation of the circumstances of Laius's death, reveals the long hidden identity of his murderer. Like Socrates's, Oedipus's "wisdom" is a kind of knowledge, but what this second piece of knowledge reveals, however, is that, unlike Socrates, Oedipus is remarkable for the most important thing he does *not* know: the truth of his own identity. As Teiresias points out to Oedipus (*Oedipus Tyrannus* 366–67, for example), Oedipus has no knowledge or understanding of himself. Oedipus, then, in this regard stands in exactly the opposite situation to Socrates. This is underlined, too, by the first distinctive piece of knowledge that Oedipus possesses: the nature of "man" that Oedipus recognizes is the person seen from the outside, whereas Socrates's self-knowledge is precisely a matter of the person known from the inside.

By casting the story of Socrates in the terms of the story of Oedipus, Plato has given us a powerful structure for interpreting the "mythic," heroic status of Socrates. Through his writing, Plato presents myth come alive and walking among us: in Socrates Plato has embedded the hero in our lived world. He stands forth not as some lost unattainable miracle but as a human being, our fellow-citizen, our neighbor, who participates in that old transcendent glory because he did human things in a human way. Plato has brought myth into the streets, which is exactly what Plato tells us Socrates did for philosophy. At the same time, however, he is redefining the very significance of the hero, by replacing the self-ignorant, fate-governed Oedipus with the self-knowing, self-responsible Socrates. In addition to using traditional story forms to elevate the figure of the philosopher to heroic status, to making the philosopher the new hero, Plato's identification of Socrates and Oedipus also makes a statement about the nature of tradition itself.

Both Oedipus and Socrates receive an utterance from Apollo of Delphi, from a voice, that is, of long-standing, all-encompassing authority. Trust in the god's utterances is a feature of life in every city and region of Greece and the Aegean. Oedipus and Socrates both obey the god, and both are shaped by their responses to their oracles. But whereas Oedipus obeys by hearing the god's words, presuming he understands them and acting automatically and reactively to them, Socrates obeys the god by trying to learn what they mean. The explicit way that Apollo speaks and the self-conscious obedience given him parallel the implicit way that traditions speak and the unconscious obedience given them. Oedipus's reaction to the oracle parallels that of the individual who lives in tradition without scrutinizing or understanding it; for such an individual, tradition dictates certain responses that people appropriately and automatically make. Socrates's response to the oracle suggests another attitude to tradition: it suggests a self-conscious struggle to understand the import of tradition and recognition of the essentiality of one's own role in taking up what the world hands one. In celebrating Socrates as the new hero,

Plato is also championing a new attitude to tradition, an attitude he himself evinces in his creative use of traditional means—the myth of Oedipus—to tell a new story.

There is a further, final difference between Socrates and Oedipus that is highlighted by the distinctive ways in which each is transformed by his devotion to Apollo. While Oedipus is transformed from a polluted Theban resister of Apollo into an Athenian *polis*-hero, Socrates first becomes an interpreter of Apollo (23b) and then becomes a self-described prophet—a *mantis*—of Apollo. As we saw above, Socrates, after receiving the sentence of death, prophesies to the Athenians about the dangers they have created for themselves by deciding to destroy the gift of a god: he describes himself specifically and precisely as "speaking as an oracle"—*chrēsmōidein* (39c)—and "speaking like a prophet"—*manteuesthai* (39d). In his depiction of himself as a prophet, Socrates resembles, in particular, another prominent character from Sophocles's *Oedipus Tyrannus:* Teiresias of Thebes, the most renowned prophet of Apollo in Greek myth. Let us look, finally, at the way in which Plato's identification of Socrates with Teiresias leaves behind the world of Sophoclean myth and places Socrates in the more universal domain of Homeric myth.

Teiresias

As we turn to the end of the *Apology*, we see Socrates, condemned to death, speculating about what death will be. He does not fear death, he says, but looks forward to meeting all the famous people in Hades. He describes those whom he expects to find there (41a–c): the judges of the dead, Minos, Rhadamanthus, Aeacus, and Triptolemus; the great poets, Orpheus, Musaeus, Homer, and Hesiod; the great heroes of the Trojan cycle of myth, Palamedes, Telamonian Ajax, Agamemnon, Odysseus, and the notorious Sisyphus. The figures he lists are predominantly figures we meet in Homeric epic.[12] Odysseus is, of course, the hero of the *Odyssey*. Several others appear in the *Odyssey* in Book 11, which describes Odysseus's trip to the land of the dead. Agamemnon appears at *Odyssey* 11.385–464, Telamonian Ajax at 11.541–67, Minos at 11.568–71, and Sisyphus at 11.593–600. According to the *Odyssey*, Rhadamanthus does not preside over the dead, but over the blessed heroes who are taken to Elysium (4.563–69); nonetheless, he is still mentioned by the poem. Aeacus is not a character in the Homeric poems, but his name appears frequently as a patronymic epithet of Achilleus, Aeacides;[13] Aeacus is a son of Zeus and Achilleus's grandfather (*Iliad* 21.187–89). Palamedes is a figure from the now-fragmentary epic poem the *Cypria*, attributed to

Homer or Stasinus; the *Cypria* focuses on Helen's abduction by Paris. In it, Palamedes is drowned by Odysseus and Diomedes (*Cypria* fragment 21). Triptolemus is mentioned in the *Homeric Hymn to Demeter* (153, 473–79) as one of the four kings of Eleusis.

When Socrates describes his own possible afterlife, then, he does it in terms that place him fairly firmly in a Homeric setting. His inclusion of Agamemnon, Telamonian Ajax, Minos, and Sisyphus, in particular, evokes Book 11 of the *Odyssey,* which contains Odysseus's account of his own journey to the land of the dead. That journey was made for the sole purpose of consulting the shade of the Theban prophet Teiresias, who is supposed to be able to tell Odysseus how to get home to Ithaca (*Odyssey* 10.490–95). Teiresias we have met in another instantiation in *Oedipus Tyrannus,* where he was remarkable for his ability to know and understand the truth, aided by his gift of prophecy from Apollo. Teiresias in the *Odyssey* is outstanding among the shades because his mind is *steadfast* (he has *phrenes empedoi*); he alone has intelligence and sense when all the others are flittering shadows, a gift from Persephone herself (10.493–95). He manifests this superior understanding when he, alone of the shades with whom Odysseus converses, knows Odysseus and speaks to him before he has tasted of the revivifying mixture Odysseus has prepared for the dead (11.93–97).[14] Teiresias, then, is marked in death, as he was in life, by having knowledge and understanding beyond the norm. In death *he knows who he is* when no one else does. The dead in the *Odyssey* exist in a world of mist and inactivity. They have no consciousness, no self-consciousness. They return to themselves briefly when Odysseus allows them to drink from his trench filled with honey, milk, wine, water, and barley (11.24–28), but otherwise are, really, shadows. Dead, Teiresias alone is just who he was when alive, and he alone, dead, acts just as he acted when alive.

When Socrates draws upon the Homeric myths, then, we find in Teiresias a figure already provided by the tradition who is like Socrates, just as we found in Oedipus a traditional figure like Socrates the investigator. The most definitive textual identification here is the insistence of the *Odyssey* that Teiresias in death remains just as he was in life. Socrates likewise insists that he will be in death just what he was in life. He will go around questioning the dead, "just as he did the living" (41b). This portrayal of Socrates also implies that he will also be like Teiresias in that his mind will be steadfast: he will have intelligence and sense. This identification with Teiresias is then cemented by Socrates describing himself as a servant and *mantis* of Apollo who prophesies for the Athenians their future without him. The comparison with Teiresias is framed in terms of Socrates's death, but most of all the Homeric image of Teiresias reminds us of what Socrates's *life* has been. Like

Teiresias among the shades, Socrates in his life has been the only one who has had awareness of himself and of the truth of his life: Socrates's quest to refute the oracle ended up by giving him a distinctive understanding of himself apparently shared by no one else, and his service to the god turned him into someone who stood alone in the clarity of his understanding in a world full of others blinded by the fog of their own ignorance, conceit, and laziness.

In *Oedipus Tyrannus,* Teiresias's true prophecies are not heeded, and his speaking truly in fact earns him the anger of Oedipus. Socrates's gift, too, has been his curse and, even as he looks forward to continuing to benefit from this gift, we readers of the Homeric epic and of the *Apology* have to think that Socrates's future will indeed be like his life, if, like Teiresias, he goes to the poet's Hades to pursue his old ways and to be surrounded by flittering shadows, despite the fact that, as Socrates notes, the dead do not kill people for conversation.[15]

Tragedy to Epic

Throughout the previous discussion of Socrates and Oedipus, I have insisted on Socrates's ties, not to the traditional mythic figure of Oedipus in general, but his ties to one particular instantiation of this traditional figure, the version we find in Sophocles's two extant Oedipus plays. Sophocles wrote and produced these two plays for performance at the great festival of Dionysus in Athens during the fifth century B.C.E. His version of Oedipus appears to be, as far as the remains of earlier poetry tells us, a fifth-century Athenian innovation in several respects. The earliest version of Oedipus available to us appears in archaic epic; the *Odyssey* tells us that Oedipus's mother, Epicasta, marries her son, but dies soon after the marriage once the gods make the truth of the incest known (11.279–80); there is no mention of any children produced by this relationship. Other archaic sources do mention children of Oedipus, but they are produced with his second wife, usually identified as Astymedousa, daughter of Sthenelus. The first secure source for Oedipus and his mother having children together is Aeschylus's *Seven Against Thebes,* produced in Athens in the early 460s. Oedipus's killing his father is traditional. Earlier versions of Oedipus myth seem uniformly to portray Oedipus as dying at Thebes and dying as an honored king in battle; so, for example, *Iliad* 23.677–80 mentions that the hero Mecisteus participates in the funeral games for the fallen Oedipus at Thebes; "fallen" (*dedoupōn*) in epic poetry generally refers to those killed in battle. Funeral games are held for kings and great heroes, not for criminals and exiles.

Oedipus's exile from Thebes is first hinted at by Sophocles's *Oedipus Tyrannus,* produced sometime between 440 and 419. Teiresias tells Oedipus that the murderer of Laius will travel blind to a strange land (454–56), and Oedipus demands that Creon expel him from the city, but Creon demurs, wanting to wait until he has consulted the will of the gods (1435–39). The play thus ends with the fate of Oedipus left hanging. The first certain references to the complete story of Oedipus sent into exile, received by Theseus in Athens, and dead in Athens are found in the last decade of the fifth century in Euripides's *Phoenissae* and in Sophocles's *Oedipus at Colonus.* This innovative Athenian Oedipus has become "our" Oedipus largely because of the vagaries of the preservation of ancient texts and because of the preeminence of Sophocles's plays; other versions that did not follow the new path set by the Athenian dramatists continued to be told in the ancient world.

In the *Apology,* then, Plato is tying Socrates's career, not to myth and tradition in general, but to Athenian fifth-century myth in particular. He is using local myth to articulate his account of a local hero. The local myth of Oedipus, designed for performance at the Great Dionysia, is in essence democratic myth.[16] One of the goals of fifth-century Athenian tragedy is to promote democratic Athenian ideology. Among the many manifestations of this goal, we see repeatedly that the great aristocratic heroes of epic and earlier myth are portrayed as ultimately destructive and intolerable in a city-state.[17] Plato's heroizing of Socrates in the *Apology* follows a typical Athenian pattern: the hero is admirable, noble, sympathetic, but ultimately must be destroyed for the *polis* to be and feel safe. Socrates's devotion to his kind of philosophy, the life of examining and testing his citizens, is regarded by democratic Athenians as destructive, idiosyncratic, and worthy only of eradication. Through this eradication, the city tells itself that everything will be fine now that Socrates is gone.[18]

Plato's Socrates does not end his career in the *Apology* as the Athenian Oedipus, though. Plato is not content to leave Athenians self-satisfied with their elimination of the hero, and the critique of this Athenian "hero-busting" mythology is communicated not only explicitly through Socrates's manifest words of self-defense, but also implicitly through casting Socrates as the new Teiresias. As we have seen, the language in which Socrates describes himself as a prophet situates him distinctively in the domain of archaic epic. This transformation thereby moves the figure of Socrates from the myths belonging to Athens and her democracy into the more universal and traditional (and aristocratic) world of pan-Hellenic myth. Unlike tragedy, Homeric epic regards itself as having an audience that consists of all Greeks at all times:

one of its goals is to speak to a ruling class throughout Greece that identified with and aspired to the values of the great heroes of epic poetry.[19] Moving Socrates out of Athenian myth and into epic myth precisely challenges the idea that the local perspective of Athens and its laws is sufficient to define the terms for assessing the reality that is Socrates. In presenting him as belonging to the world of old heroes like Achilleus, Odysseus, Heracles, and Oedipus— a world to which his idiosyncrasy, his single-minded pursuit of his quest, and his neglect of all other aspects of his life clearly belong—Plato in fact uses an older, aristocratic tradition (which might otherwise appear conservative or reactionary) precisely to point to the need for new values, a new universality that extends beyond the limited values of Athens and her democratic ideology. It is precisely by casting his hero in the terms of the past that Plato calls for the need for a new future.

Genre and Innovation

Attic tragedy and Homeric epic provide the rhetorical materials for the *Apology*, but the *Apology* is itself a significantly different genre of storytelling than either. The *Apology* purports to be a text of three speeches given by Socrates at his trial for impiety in Athens. Throughout the text, with the exception of Socrates's cross-examination of Meletus, Socrates's is the only voice. He is the narrator of his own history, the expounder of his stance toward his present situation, and the prophet of his own future. Socrates is, in essence, the bard who performs his own mythic tale. In tragedy, the poet is self-effacing: he does not appear onstage *in propria persona*, he does not speak for himself, but appears only through the medium of his characters and his chorus. In epic poetry, there is an identifiable first-person narrator: Hesiod speaks for himself; names himself; has opinions, a past, and a family; and calls on the Muses for assistance. Homer likewise calls on the Muses for help at crucial points in his narrative, addresses characters in the second person, and the like. The bard of epic poetry sings the praise of heroes but makes his presence and his power felt constantly. In the *Apology*, Socrates unites the role of bard and hero. Socrates's bardic status manifests itself not just in his being the one who does all of the talking; Socrates also manifests the key feature that traditionally defines bardic inspiration by the Muses: knowledge. According to Hesiod's *Theogony*, the Muses give the bard power to sing the things that are, the things that were, and the things that will be: the present, the past, and the future (*Theogony* 32; compare *Iliad* 2.485–92), and it is precisely this that Socrates purports to be able to sing as he authoritatively tells the story of his own heroic life. Socrates's three speeches are devoted to the past (his original accusers and his life story), the present (his assessment of an appropriate penalty once he has been found guilty), and the future (his prophecies about his own life after death and about what will happen in Athens once he has died). In telling his own past, present, and future, Socrates becomes the ultimate self-conscious epic bard.

Plato, though, is the writer of the *Apology*. His story is the story of the hero who is the self-conscious bard, the hero who can tell his own story: the hero defined by knowing himself. Plato himself, though, is like the poet of tragedy: he does not appear himself as such, but effaces himself in the manifest self-presentation of his characters. It is Plato's use of traditional story forms that allows Socrates to appear in this way, and, in thus presenting Socrates in traditional forms, Plato shows that the very ability to be autobiographical rests in the traditional forms for self-interpretation. Plato's writing presents us with a new hero—the philosophical autobiographer, the self-knower— and with a new genre—the Platonic dialogue, in which traditional genres are themselves creatively transformed to release meanings they did not themselves anticipate.

The *Apology*, then, does considerably more than allude to myth, to "what the poets say." Plato is rather a devotee of myth, as Socrates is a devotee of Apollo, struggling to understand the real significance of the myths he inherited in and through the same process by which he uses those myths to express the unique meanings demanded by his situation. In a very specific way, he has used the myth of Oedipus in its Athenian version to underscore the nature of Socrates's pursuit of understanding and the nature of the Athenians' decision to execute him; democratic Athens cannot recognize a hero when it sees one.[20] Even more, though, what Plato has achieved in the *Apology* is a profound reworking of mythic thought.[21] He demonstrates that he is as fully imbued with mythic-poetic thinking as Sophocles or the Homeric bards, and he exploits the meanings immanent in traditional narrative structures so powerfully that his own hero, Socrates, really does, for us, live up to the definition of myth as traditional tale with which I began: Plato's Socrates is not merely a story, not merely an image of the past, but is a setting of the terms for articulating reality in a way that ongoingly structures our very way of making sense of our world.

CHAPTER 6

The *Crito* and Thersites

Near the beginning of the *Crito,* Socrates explains to Crito why he does not think that the sacred ship (after whose arrival in Athens Socrates will be executed) will be arriving on the present day. He has had a dream, he says, in which a beautiful and shapely woman in white robes called to him and said, "Socrates, on the third day you might arrive in fertile Phthia" (*ēmati ken tritatōi Phthiēn eribōlon hikoio*) (*Crito* 44a5–b2). We shall see that this line, when embedded in Socrates's dream in *Crito,* is open to different interpretations: superficially, it is about traveling to Phthia, in Thessaly; most importantly, it points to an identification of Socrates and Achilleus. This line is a slightly altered quotation of a line spoken by Achilleus in Book 9 of the *Iliad,* "On the third day I might arrive in fertile Phthia" (*ēmati ke tritatōi Phthiēn eribōlon hikoimēn*) (*Iliad* 9.363). Socrates has changed the person of the verb, rendering a statement made by Achilleus about himself in *Iliad* 9 a statement made by the beautiful woman about Socrates; Socrates in *Crito,* then, is likening himself to the Achilleus of *Iliad* 9. I will demonstrate in this chapter that, as we saw with the Athenian Stranger's quoting of the *Odyssey* in *Laws* 2, when Plato quotes the line of the *Iliad* in *Crito,* he calls into active presence the context of this line and the themes at work in this context, in particular the question of remaining in place or staying.

I shall begin by laying out the context in which Achilleus utters this line in *Iliad* 9, to understand what the terms are in which Socrates casts his situation by invoking this quotation. We will see that Socrates is presenting himself as facing the choice of Achilleus, to retreat from Troy and live a long life, or to die for the sake of his heroic project. In the dialogue, Crito endeavors to persuade Socrates to flee from the jail in Athens and take refuge with associates of Crito in Thessaly. He recommends that Socrates, like Achilleus in the *Iliad,* consider turning his back on his "heroic" project: his life project of doing philosophy. Crito thereby demonstrates that he fundamentally misunderstands Socrates and, indeed, dishonors him. In this recommendation and dishonoring Crito reveals himself to be very much like another advocate of flight, Thersites, who, in *Iliad* 2 advises the Achaeans to leave Troy to return to Greece. Crito, then, is to Socrates as Thersites is to the Achaeans, offering advice that dishonors and misrepresents those he claims to advise. In *Crito*, Plato thus has Crito and Socrates reenact one of the most resonant moments of traditional meaning that the Greeks possessed, but in such a way as to celebrate a very different kind of hero than the heroes of the *Iliad*.[1] Through Socrates's rebuttal of Crito's advice, first in argument and then in the story of Socrates's conversation with the laws of Athens, Plato reveals the "heroic" character of Socrates's commitment to philosophy, and his unique and creative relationship to Athens and her laws.

Socrates's Dream

The line Socrates quotes from *Iliad* 9 appears a little less than halfway through a long speech that Achilleus makes in response to a speech by Odysseus. At this point in the poem, Achilleus has been withdrawn from the fighting long enough for the Trojans to have had such success on the battlefield that they have decided, for the first time in almost ten years of war, to spend the night camped on the plain outside the walls of Troy rather than withdraw into the city (*Iliad* 8.497–565). This display of Trojan confidence so distresses Agamemnon that he summons a council of elders at which the group decides to send an embassy to Achilleus to attempt to persuade him to return to the fighting (*Iliad* 9.89–181). The three ambassadors are Phoenix, the old friend of Achilleus; Telamonian Ajax; and Odysseus (*Iliad* 9.168–69). Agamemnon, wishing to make their appeal to Achilleus more persuasive, offers him not only the young woman Briseis (the prize Agamemnon takes from Achilleus in Book 1, as a result of which Achilleus withdraws from battle), but also precious objects, horses, more women, a chief share in the spoils of Troy, and, should they all get safely back to Greece, marriage with whichever one of Agamemnon's daughters he chooses, along with a dowry of seven cities currently under Agamemnon's control (*Iliad* 9.120–56). When the embassy arrives at Achilleus's encampment, they first receive appropriate hospitality from Achilleus (*Iliad* 9.205–21). Odysseus then speaks. He tells Achilleus that the fate of the Achaeans is doubtful as long as Achilleus holds himself off from the fighting, since the Trojans and their allies now are camped out on the plain, eager to fall on the Achaean ships and set them on fire (*Iliad* 9.230–46). He asks Achilleus to return to the fighting and defend the Achaeans, giving up his anger (*cholos*) (*Iliad* 9.247–60). He then lists for Achilleus all of the gifts offered by Agamemnon, repeating Agamemnon's list almost verbatim (*Iliad* 9.261–99).[2] He concludes his speech with a request that Achilleus, even if he hates Agamemnon, pity the rest of the Achaeans and drive the Trojans away from the ships (*Iliad* 9.300–306). It is at this point that Achilleus makes the speech in which the line quoted by Socrates appears.

Achilleus's response to Odysseus's speech with its offer of gifts from Agamemnon is to become angry and to reject the idea that Agamemnon or any of the Achaeans will persuade him to return to the fighting (*Iliad* 9.315–19). He announces that on the following day, having offered sacrifices to Zeus and the rest of the gods, he and his men will get into their ships and sail home; if they meet with good weather, he says, uttering the line Socrates quotes, on the third day Achilleus will arrive in Phthia (*Iliad* 9.356–63). Achilleus tells the embassy that he left much wealth behind at home and that he will bring much spoil back with him (*Iliad* 9.364–67). He rejects Agamemnon's gifts and his offer of marriage to one of Agamemnon's daughters (*Iliad* 9.378–90). His father, Peleus, will find him a bride in Greece when he gets home (*Iliad* 9.393–97). He tells the delegation that his mother, Thetis, told him that if he stays at Troy to fight he will win glory but lose his homecoming, whereas if he goes home he will have no glory but will live for a long time (*Iliad* 9.410–16). He dismisses the ambassadors but bids Phoenix to remain with him so that he can accompany Achilleus home the next day (*Iliad* 9.421–29).[3]

The Achilleus Socrates quotes, then, is an Achilleus resolved to abandon his heroic project, the Trojan War, and to go to Phthia, where he will live a long and uneventful life. But, as readers of the *Iliad* know, and as Socrates knows, Achilleus, despite his threat, does not return home to Phthia. He stays at Troy to see his vengeance on Agamemnon through; he returns to battle after the death of his companion Patroclus in Book 16 and ultimately ends up dying at Troy himself. Socrates's dream quotes Achilleus at a moment of crisis; in *Iliad* 9 Achilleus must decide whether to stay at Troy and complete the heroic project to which he has devoted his life or to go home and give up on being the hero Achilleus in favor of being the obscure old man Achilleus.

Through his quotation of *Iliad* 9, then, Socrates tells us that he is himself facing the situation of Achilleus: he will have to decide whether to continue his lifelong philosophical project and remain in Athens to face death or to escape and give up on that project for the sake of continuing to live. Through his accurate quotation of a line from the *Iliad,* demonstrating his precise knowledge of the material, Socrates implicitly claims that he must now himself make the famous "choice of Achilleus."

Socrates's self-conscious knowledge of and engagement with the *Iliad* here are quite different from Crito's response to the quotation and the dream.

Socrates's quote is an indication of Socrates's clear critical awareness of the precise nature of the situation that faces him. Crito, on the other hand, appears deaf to any meaning implicit in the dream. He shows no awareness that this quotation carries any meaning other than the meaning that Socrates claims to put upon it when he says that the dream shows that he will die in two days. Crito acknowledges that Socrates takes the dream in that particular way and then plunges into his attempts to persuade Socrates to flee Athens (44b). Crito does not appear to see—at all—that what he proposes to Socrates (escape from Athens and execution) is that Socrates make a choice analogous to Achilleus's choice, a choice between remaining himself, committed to what he has always valued, and abandoning himself, ignoring what he has always valued.[4]

Crito and Thersites

What Crito attempts as he tries to persuade Socrates to escape from prison is to persuade Socrates to turn his back on his lifelong philosophical project (as Socrates makes clear to him in their conversation from 46b onward). For Crito, it is more important simply to remain alive than to die for the values one lives by—the precise view Socrates rejected in the *Apology* and, indeed, in his whole life. Crito assumes that Socrates will share this view and so attempts to persuade him to disregard the laws of Athens and to flee. Crito's behavior in this passage (his misinterpretation of Socrates, his advocacy of the abandonment of the project), brings into play another Iliadic episode: the speech of Thersites before the Achaeans in *Iliad* 2. In this episode, we see another exhortation to flee and abandon a heroic project, and the stern rejection of that proposal.

In *Iliad* 2, Agamemnon attempts to test the Achaeans by falsely telling them that he had a dream that advised him to return home.[5] When the assembled Achaeans hear of this dream, they rise in disorder from their seats and rush toward their ships to go home. Odysseus with the help of Athene manages to drive the Achaeans back to assembly. Once they are all back in their places, Thersites rises and speaks. Thersites is, the *Iliad* says, the *aischistos*—the ugliest, most vile and shameful—man to come to Troy (*Iliad* 2.216). Thersites is a speaker of abuse (*oneidea*) and strife (*neikea*) against kings, and he seeks to make the Achaeans laugh through his ridicule (*Iliad* 2.212–22).[6] From the perspective of Homeric poetry, he is not a speaker of things that are true and lasting, like the *Iliad* and the *Odyssey*, but a speaker of inaccuracy who aims to harm with his words rather than to commemorate.[7] Thersites urges retreat.

Thersites begins his speech at the assembly by abusing Agamemnon, asking him at which Achaean he is now angry, and goes on to remind him how rich he is in battle spoil (*Iliad* 2.226–28). He urges the Achaeans to return home, since it is unmanly for them to fight for a leader as greedy and exploitive as Agamemnon (*Iliad* 2.235–38). His abuse of Agamemnon spreads to include all the Achaeans; he addresses the Achaeans at 2.235 as "base objects of reproach, Achaean women, no longer Achaeans" (*kak' elenche', Achaiïdes, ouket' Achaioi*). The speech ends with Thersites reminding the assembly how Agamemnon has dishonored Achilleus, who is much better (*meg' ameinona*) than Agamemnon (*Iliad* 2.239–40). Once Thersites is finished speaking, Odysseus stands up, rebukes him (*Iliad* 2.246–64), and strikes him (*Iliad* 2.265–66). Thersites begins to weep and sits down, trembling (*Iliad* 2.268–69), while the Achaeans laugh and say what a good thing Odysseus has done (*Iliad* 2.270–77).

Thersites's words are called, by the poem, *oneidos* and *neikos* (*Iliad* 2.222, 224, 243), abuse and blame. His words are, then, *interpreting* words that take a stance toward the events they describe. As abuse and blame, these words seek to find fault, to impute base motives, and to treat Agamemnon (the object of Thersites's *neikos*) as someone who does wrong and who does wrong only for bad reasons. They seek to abuse the Achaeans as a group, calling them base and effeminate. Thersites portrays everyone as worthy of blame.[8]

Thersites's abusive words are also expressive of aspects of his own character. Most significantly here, Thersites urges the Achaeans to sail home, to abandon the attempt to sack Troy. He advises that they all turn their backs on the heroic project to which they have dedicated themselves for almost ten years, that they give up on the possibility of accomplishing that project. Thersites advocates withdrawal from fighting and flight home: in the eyes of the *Iliad,* he gives the advice of a coward.

In his rebuke, Odysseus reiterates the view that Thersites is the most shameful, ugly, and cowardly man who came to Troy, saying that no man more inferior or less brave (*cheiroteron*) came with Agamemnon to Troy (*Iliad* 2.248–49). Thersites's behavior after Odysseus rebukes and strikes him bears out these descriptions. He does not stand up to Odysseus, and he does not defend himself. He starts to cry and immediately is silenced and put back into his place. Thersites behaves like a coward, refusing to stand to account for his words and his behavior.[9] He avoids further unpleasant consequences by disappearing into the crowd. His advice to the Achaeans is, in essence, to do the same thing: retreat from Troy now rather than see your project through to its end, avoid the further unpleasantness of battle and being away from home. He advises that the Achaeans become like him.

Thersites, then, out of his cowardly and abusive stance, recommends the abandoning of the entire heroic project that has occupied both Trojans and Achaeans for almost ten years and the war that provides the subject matter for the *Iliad*. Claiming to give advice at the assembly, Thersites demonstrates his ignorance of and hostility to what drives the Achaeans, what drives the *Iliad*. As someone who cannot understand what motivates heroes, Thersites easily advises heroes to turn their backs on their heroic commitments.

At the beginning of the *Crito*, Crito is in a position with respect to Socrates similar to that of Therites with respect to the Achaeans. Like Thersites, Crito advises that his hero, Socrates, turn his back on his heroic project and flee the place where he will die.[10] As he attempts to justify this advice and persuade Socrates to follow it, Crito demonstrates that, as much as he claims to be speaking out of sympathy and concern for Socrates, he does not understand who Socrates is or what he believes. The advice he offers is not advice that could possibly move Socrates because it does not *speak to* Socrates but to some false image of Socrates.[11] Indeed, Crito's advice assumes that Socrates was never serious in the past when he said what he said and did what he did. Crito treats Socrates's commitments as simply dismissable, worth as little to Socrates as they are to Crito. Only by misinterpreting and misrepresenting Socrates, just as Thersites misinterprets and misrepresents the Achaeans, can Crito offer the arguments that he does. Let us look at Crito's behavior.

Crito begins with Crito sitting next to Socrates early in the morning. Socrates wakes up after Crito has been in his cell with him for some time, having been unwilling, he says, to wake Socrates because he wanted him to spend his time pleasantly, in sleep (*Crito* 43b). Crito remarks that he has often considered Socrates's way of life happy, but no more than at present as he sees Socrates bearing his present misfortune easily and gently (*Crito* 43b6–9). The conversation begins, then, with Crito making a decision for Socrates (not to wake Socrates up) out of a consideration of what he, Crito, considers pleasant. To Crito, to sleep is more pleasant than to be awake and to face being in prison waiting to die. At the same time, he acknowledges that Socrates's way of living is happy and that this way of living allows Socrates to be calm and easy as he sits in prison waiting to die. Socrates's way of living has been, in part, to spend his life in conversation and not to accept without question typical ways of thinking, typical values, such as, for example, believing that dying is a bad thing, a misfortune.[12] So this conversation begins with Crito expressing admiration and affection for Socrates, but the image of "Socrates" that Crito relies upon as he leaves him to sleep is not the Socrates Crito admires. Crito's behavior already presents us—and Socrates—with a false image of Socrates, just as Thersites presented us with a false image of the

Achaeans. Crito behaves toward Socrates as though Socrates were the kind of person Crito is.

When Socrates, in response to Crito's noting that he is bearing his present misfortune easily, says that a man as old as Socrates should not be angry at dying, Crito replies that others of the same age certainly do take dying badly (*Crito* 43b10–c3). To resent impending death is, Crito notes, a common human situation; Socrates, then, should he be upset at being about to die, would be taking death in a typical way. With this comment, Crito indicates for us one of the paths his subsequent arguments will take: he expects Socrates to think and act in ways typical of people in general and of Athenian men in particular.

Crito attempts to persuade Socrates to escape from jail and flee Athens to preserve his life. Crito offers to bribe the jailers to release Socrates, and says that he has arranged for refuge for Socrates with some of his associates in Thessaly. In his persuasion, Crito appeals to principles that would be acknowledged as forceful by typical Athenian men. He claims that to remain in prison to be executed would be for Socrates to gratify his enemies. This action would be a violation of the notion that a man should help his friends and harm his enemies. Crito argues that Socrates owes it to his friends to escape from prison. Crito further argues that his own reputation will suffer if he is perceived by the people of Athens not to have done anything to get Socrates out of trouble. If Socrates remains in prison, then, he is harming Crito through harming his reputation. Finally, he tells Socrates that to remain in prison rather than to flee would be the act of a coward, because he did not do everything possible to save himself before and during his trial and after the verdict (45e–46a). Overall, then, Crito's argument amounts to a blaming of Socrates and an appeal to "received views" about how it is proper to behave.[13]

What is remarkable about Crito's attempts to persuade is that he makes these attempts, using the terms he does, knowing that Socrates is Socrates and that Socrates has spent his life pursuing wisdom, questioning the "received views," and challenging the typical. The justifications Crito puts forward for Socrates's flight are all grounded in the received and the typical and so must face the kind of scrutiny that Socrates always gives appeals to typical values.

Socrates's Response

In *Iliad* 2, Thersites purports to be speaking in sympathy with the Achaeans, but his position in fact rests in a misinterpretation, and it is countered by a forceful rejection: Odysseus tells him that he has no right to speak and hits him; Thersites retreats and sits down, and the assembled Achaeans laugh at him. Crito meets with a similarly complete rejection from Socrates.

Crito's misunderstandings and misrepresentations are answered and stopped by powerful statements that articulate and make manifest the very structures and values that he dishonors. Crito is answered first by Socrates's refutation of his arguments in favor of flight and then by Socrates's conversation with the laws of Athens, in the course of which Socrates lays out what it is that he takes to be his relationship to his city and its laws. While Crito himself gives no sign that these statements make any difference to him or change his way of thinking about Socrates's situation, for the reader these statements lay out just what Socrates's creative and *caring* relationship to Athens and her laws and traditions, her *nomoi*, are.

Crito's attempt to persuade Socrates to flee to Thessaly ends at 46a. Socrates's response is the response that any reader of Plato would expect: that he and Crito should *consider* whether he should flee or not, and that he, Socrates, is ready as always to be persuaded by that *logos* that seems best to him upon rational consideration (*hos an moi logizomenōi beltistos phanētai*) (46b2–6). He reminds Crito that he cannot now give up the *logoi* he spoke in previous times unless they now together find better *logoi* to replace them (46b6–c1). Socrates insists here, to his old friend, that he is *the same* Socrates he has always been, that he holds to the same beliefs and practices he has always held. Socrates reminds Crito of a point that he makes to the jury in the *Apology:* Socrates is self-consistent and will *always* consider the *logoi* of things, will *always* do philosophy.[14]

Socrates's rational consideration of Crito's arguments for flight is, indeed, consistent with Socrates's usual way of examining *logoi,* and it aims, in particular, to remind Crito of principles he, Crito, has formerly espoused, ultimately showing that Crito is himself failing to be self-consistent. Socrates reminds Crito of their shared past, their conversations, and the agreements they have reached about justice, knowledge, and authority.[15] He rearticulates for Crito the things he knows about Socrates and what Socrates believes and how Socrates behaves—things that should have prevented Crito's trying to persuade Socrates to flee through appeal to typical ways of thinking. Socrates would not be the person he is were he to heed Crito's advice, and Crito should already know this.

In the course of their discussion, Crito and Socrates agree that life with a damaged soul is not worth living (47e7–48a2). What damages the soul most, it emerges, is willingly to engage in injustice. Socrates demands of Crito whether he *still* agrees with this principle, which they have agreed on before;

Crito assures Socrates that he does stand by that agreement (49e4). Consequently, people should do the things they *have agreed* (*homologēsēi*, 49e6) are
just (49e5–8). The next, concluding stage of Socrates's discourse with Crito
will use this notion of agreement in a particularly powerful way. The concluding section of Socrates's answer to Crito contains Socrates's portrayal of
a conversation between himself and the laws of Athens, the *nomoi*. Socrates
asks, would it be standing by what they have agreed to go away without having persuaded the city to let them go (49e9–50a3)? When Crito is unable
even to begin to respond to this question (50a4–5), Socrates commences his
narrative of the conversation he would have with the laws, should they come
to him at this moment and question him.[16]

Socrates's representation of his possible conversation with the laws aims to
show two things. First, Socrates uses the conversation to show how it is only
with the domain of the laws that he—or anyone else, for that matter—can
be the person he is. Second, Socrates uses the conversation to show that the
laws are themselves dependent upon the particular, personal adherence and
care of those very individuals who depend upon them. Let us briefly consider
this second point first.

Socrates has the laws ask how they can possibly continue to exist and
function when individuals refuse to abide by and recognize as authoritative
the verdicts of the city's law courts (50b2–5). If a private individual can simply ignore the verdict of one of the city's law courts, then the verdict has
no force, and the law court and the law that lie behind the verdict are not
sovereign, not authoritative, not *kuriai*. They are not law. For law to exist in
Athens, the citizens must act as though bound by the law; if they do not do
so, then law does not exist. The force of law, in other words, exists only insofar
as individuals allow it to exist.[17]

After considering this dependence of the laws upon individuals, Socrates's
story of his conversation with the laws focuses on the dependence of individuals upon the laws. The personified laws explain the constitutive role that
the laws of Athens have played in making Socrates be the Socrates that he is.
Socrates's account of his relationship to Athens and her laws begins with an
account of *everyone's* relationship with the *nomoi* under which they grew up.
The *nomoi* are like our parents in that they shape and determine our world,
govern our behavior and our understanding, before we can ever be aware that
they do these things. They are not optional parts of our world about which
we have a choice: they build us, nourish us, and guide us through life, in a
way analogous to the way that our parents build us to speak, to interact with
others, to deal with food in particular ways, and so on. It is by living in the
context of the laws that we develop the very ability to speak, to think, and,

indeed, to choose. The authority of the *nomoi,* thus, is not simply the explicit authority of command and obedience; it is the authority of way of life, of tradition, of habit.[18] And in most situations the *force* of law is not an explicit intervention to direct our behavior; the force of law, rather, is of such long standing that the very form of our behavior is, simply, law-abiding. Socrates's point here is that the laws provide for all people the structures and, indeed, the content *through* which they will live their lives: laws are not external to us, but are the essential, formative context of our identities.

In these aspects, Socrates's account of the laws so far is an account of the roles of any *nomoi* in the lives of those who belong to them. We begin to see some of the distinctly democratic Athenian aspects of these *nomoi* when Socrates has the laws say that those who do not find them just are free to try to persuade the *nomoi* to alter their understanding of what is just. *These* laws are not monolithic, but responsive to the citizens whose job it is to enact them; that is, citizens can gather and decide together to change their laws according to their changing needs and their changing sense of what is just and good. The laws need to remain relevant to (which is to say, just for) their citizens. We see from this discussion that laws are dependent upon their citizens to keep them alive, not only in the sense indicated above of, for example, abiding by the rulings of the law courts, by preserving the laws as they are, but also *by carrying them ahead into the future,* shaped appropriately to be meaningful in that future. In democratic Athens, citizens must be engaged with understanding and engaging with their laws, and thereby enacting and keeping those laws authoritative. Those recognized as citizens have access to all of the benefits of citizenship, have been made into citizens through the auspices of the city's institutions, and have the responsibility of keeping the city, her institutions, and her laws functional *and just.* Citizens like Socrates, who approach law and institutions generally with the critical demand that they be laws and institutions *of justice,* bring the city and her *nomoi* into something like a relationship of reciprocal care and recognition.

Having laid out for Crito the kind of relationship that any Athenian should have to the city and the *nomoi,* Socrates goes on to lay out the nature of his own particular relationship with Athens and the *nomoi.* He has the laws point out that Socrates, more than any other Athenian, has freely given his assent to the laws of Athens not only through his continuing as an adult to live in Athens but also through having almost never left the city over the course of his life (52b). He has also chosen to have children and to raise them in Athens under its laws (52c). Moreover, once he was found guilty at his trial, he did not propose exile as a counter penalty when the prosecution proposed execution (52e). Of Athenians now living, then, Socrates has proved himself to be the *most* law-abiding, the most content with the city and the *nomoi*. His consent to the laws is not merely tacit and implicit: he has proclaimed his preference for his city openly at his trial; he has married and had children and freely chosen to remain in Athens to raise them and to have the city and its *nomoi* raise them. Socrates shows Crito that Socrates has never chosen a life other than a life under Athenian *nomoi* and that he cannot now, if he is still self-consistently Socrates, choose another.[19]

Socrates's story of his conversation with the laws concludes with Socrates setting out what will actually happen to him if he accepts Crito's advice and flees Athens. If he chooses to flee into exile, Socrates will flee as someone who is an enemy (*polemios*) to the laws and constitutions of any other city (53b4–8).[20] He will have revealed himself as someone who abides by the laws only as long as it is convenient to him so to do, but who will ignore and flout the law when he chooses; he will be revealed as someone for whom law is a convenience rather than a guiding structure. Being such a man will also mean that Socrates's ability to do philosophy will be seriously undermined (53c). Socrates could no longer seriously claim, as he now does, that excellence, justice, and institutions and laws are the most valuable things for human beings (*hē aretē kai hē dikaiosunē pleistou axion tois anthrōpois kai ta nomima kai hoi nomoi*) (53c7–9). His behavior will have manifestly demonstrated that none of these things is more valuable to him than his own skin. More significantly, Socrates's ability to continue to be the Socrates he has always been will be gone. Socrates will no longer be self-consistent; his behavior will be opposed to his words.

So what is at stake for Socrates in remaining in Athens to undergo his legally mandated execution is *the very fact of Athens* and *the very fact of Socrates*. He shows Crito through his refutation of Crito's appeal to the many and through his conversation with the laws that he, Socrates, is now in prison the same Socrates he has always been: self-consistently committed to philosophical examination of the most important human things—excellence, justice, and institutions and laws—and convinced as always that for people to do wrong is also for those people to harm themselves in their souls, in their very capacity to think, feel, and act justly. Likewise, he explains for Crito how Athens and her nurturing and guiding institutions, which have upheld and directed him throughout his life, depend upon *his* adherence to the laws and upon the adherence of all citizens; this adherence, further, is one that Socrates himself has given freely and self-consciously. To leave Athens now, following Crito's advice, would be to destroy Athens, her laws, and Socrates.[21]

Faced with Socrates's forceful articulation of the values he has challenged, Crito appears to do nothing other than acquiesce to Socrates's arguments.

Crito, when Socrates tells him that he can hear and believe nothing other than what the laws have told him,[22] can only reply that he can say nothing to that (*Crito* 54d3–9). He does not provide any evidence that he has now understood and accepted the values he previously challenged. Again, Crito appears quite unself-conscious in his relationship to tradition: because he does not critically *understand* his tradition, because he has not done what Socrates has done (creatively to examine the values and institutions of Athens), when tradition asserts itself before him he yields, but he does not particularly identify with what confronts him. Having no clear understanding of tradition in the first place, he similarly does not change his understanding but simply gives way before the weight and force of what he challenged.[23]

The Philosopher and the Hero

What we have seen, then, is that the *Crito* portrays a Socrates faced with a momentous decision analogous, as the quotation from *Iliad* 9 indicates, to the choice of Achilleus. That Socrates must make this decision comes about because Crito, Socrates's old and beloved friend, does Socrates the dishonor of treating him as though he is someone who would consider ignoring the verdict from his trial and fleeing from Athens. Crito's attempt to persuade Socrates to escape, I have argued, is like the shameful Thersites's advice to the Achaeans to flee Troy in *Iliad* 2: both derive from a failure to understand and acknowledge whom they are dealing with. Thersites cannot understand what motivates heroes; Crito cannot understand what motivates the philosopher Socrates. *Crito* lays out for us the problems inherent in Crito's notion that he can advise Socrates when he does not understand Socrates.

In a fundamental way, then, the *Crito* reenacts a traditional element of Athenian cultural meaning, and we thus see here again Plato's embedding of *his* meaning within the received terms of his tradition. The story of Socrates and Crito, that is, replays one of the definitive stories of heroism as defined by the *Iliad*. At the same time, however, Plato has shown that it is precisely the philosopher Socrates who "lives up to" this traditional meaning: it is philosophy, the commitment to self-conscious critical thinking, that is the heroic project pursued to the point of death. Plato assimilates his philosopher to the mythic warrior-hero Achilleus and thereby shows that philosophy is now the proper activity of the new hero, Socrates. Plato does not make this point by arguing *explicitly* for it; rather, drawing on a traditional poetic way of meaning through immanence, through bringing the themes of flight and heroism from *Iliad* 9 and 2 actively into play in *Crito*, Plato writes in a traditional Greek mythic-poetic way and invites a traditional Greek mythic-poetic way of reading. Plato takes up the tools that tradition has handed him and uses them to show how, in Socrates, the tradition has been transformed.

And notice, finally, that this Platonic stance toward tradition *is precisely the stance that Socrates advocates in the Crito.* In responding to Crito, Socrates identifies the laws—the traditions in which he was raised—as constitutive of his very identity: his actions and thoughts throughout his life have been mediated by the traditions of Athens, by what has been built into him by virtue of the fact that he is an Athenian man. Socrates also reminds Crito that he, Socrates, has always been creatively, caringly, and *critically* engaged with the laws and traditions of Athens through his philosophical activity. His commitment to the *maintenance* of laws has been, then, a transformative one; he has been active and self-conscious in taking up the laws and carrying them forward meaningfully into the future. His relationship to the laws is identical in structure to the relationship toward the gods—the oracle of Apollo, in particular—that he defined and defended in the *Apology*. The project of Socratic philosophy is thus precisely the maintenance of the traditional parameters of meaning through their transformation, the very project worked out in the writing that is the Platonic dialogues.

Conclusion

This book has been divided into three parts: eros, politics, and philosophy. I have chosen these three headings because each of them represents an essential aspect of human experience, action, and endeavor. Eros is the primary moving force of the soul. Politics is the domain of human life among other humans, the arena of shared experience. Philosophy is the manifestation of human striving not to be limited by the particular and relative, but to aim more toward what is universal and absolute. Each of these three domains bears an important relationship to tradition.

On first glance, it seems that eros and philosophy have no direct relationship with tradition. Politics and the city, on the other hand, seem most obviously the proper domain of tradition. The Platonic dialogues teach otherwise. Eros, the dynamic life of the soul, is something we take up through the mediation of traditional institutions—such as the pederasty that is the subject of the *Alcibiades* I—and is dependent for its fulfillment upon cultivation; indeed, this cultivation of eros is the source of our traditions, as we saw in the *Symposium*. When this living, erotic dynamism that is the secret root of tradition is forgotten, traditions can seem like dead fixtures, open to dangerous artificial manipulation, as Socrates attempts in the *Republic*, or like rigid structures that the city can use to close itself off to the new, as in the *Laws*, or, indeed, to oppress the very life of the mind, as Athens does in its condemnation of Socrates in the *Apology*. The preservation of philosophy, however, will not come through the renunciation of tradition but, as Socrates makes clear in *Crito*, and as I have argued throughout this book, by appropriating the power of tradition to speak to the demands of the "now." Through the careful reading of these Platonic dialogues, then, we see that each of these arenas—eros, politics, and philosophy—is in a reciprocal relationship with tradition. Eros and philosophy must acknowledge and live out of the weight and ground that tradition provides. Tradition and the city must be open to the challenges and transformations that both eros and philosophy can make to them.

Plato's philosophy reveals this reciprocal relationship to us while itself enacting that relationship. Plato's writing articulates the *pathos* of the individual soul and the striving of the life of the mind, but it does this through the deployment of highly traditional resources. Plato's openness to the new is simultaneously the preservation of the old. Plato's writing is thus an activity of reenactment, a *mimēsis* in the traditional Greek sense. This definitive form of Plato's writing should itself suggest a route to a new reading of the discussion of *mimēsis* in his magnum opus, the *Republic*. But that is a task for another day.[1]

Chapter 1

1. Arguments against authentic Platonic authorship tend to ground themselves either in particular scholars' views about the interpretation of Plato (for example, Nicholas D. Smith, "Did Plato Write the *Alcibiades* I?" *Apeiron* 37 [2004]: 93–108) or in stylistic analysis (for example, R. S. Bluck, "The Origin of the *Greater Alcibiades*," *Classical Quarterly* N.S. 3, nos. 1–2 [1953]: 46–52; Pamela M. Clark, "The *Greater Alcibiades*," *Classical Quarterly* N.S. 5, nos. 3–4 [1955]: 231–40). Each of these areas is highly contentious and does not really allow for any *conclusive* findings. See Nicholas Denyer for a careful assessment of the question of the dialogue's authenticity (*Plato: Alcibiades* [Cambridge: Cambridge University Press, 2001], 14–26); Denyer concludes that Plato did in fact write the *Alcibiades* I.

2. For these "old charges," see *Apology* 18b, and see the discussion by George Gregory, "Of Socrates, Aristophanes, and Rumor," in *Reexamining Socrates in the* "Apology," ed. Patricia Fagan and John Russon (Evanston, Ill.: Northwestern University Press, 2009), 35–61.

3. As we will see repeatedly throughout this book, this is exactly the form of a traditional tale or "myth."

4. This point sits for readers of Plato in Europe and North America since the nineteenth century as central to understanding Plato, as it drives the *Apology*, which for us is the key Platonic dialogue. See John Russon for a discussion of this "hearsay" that complements strongly the argument I develop here ("The [Childish] Nature of the Soul in Plato's *Apology*," in *Reexamining Socrates in the* "Apology," Fagan and Russon, 191–208).

5. All of which learning presupposes an already well-developed knowledge of how to speak Greek.

6. In Classical Athens, adult women and minors shared the same legal status, living always under the care and authority of an adult male, their *kurios.*

7. More exactly, what Alcibiades has learned is *not* Greek as such, or Greekness as such—he has learned the Greek and Greekness of a particular people in a particular place at a particular time. He is an Athenian of the late fifth century. His language is Greek, but it is the Greek of Athens as distinct from the Greek of other Greek city-states at other times. Alcibiades's Greek is both particular and universal, a "national" language in a local form.

8. For the concept of "traditional referentiality," see John Miles Foley, *Immanent Art: From Structure to Meaning in Traditional Oral Epic* (Bloomington: Indiana University Press, 1991).

9. On Athenian stereotypes of Persia, see Edith Hall, who studies the formation of the Athenian view following the Persian Wars (*Inventing the Barbarian: Greek Self-Definition Through Tragedy* [Oxford: Oxford University Press, 1989]); and Margaret C. Miller, who considers changing phases of Athenian stereotypes of Persians (*Athens and Persia in the Fifth Century BC: A Study in Cultural Receptivity* [Cambridge: Cambridge University Press, 1997]). See also Thomas Harrison for a study of the perspective embodied in Aes-

chylus's tragedy (*The Emptiness of Asia: Aeschylus' Persians and the History of the Fifth Century* [London: Duckworth, 2000]).

10. See, for example, Xenophon, *The Constitution of the Spartans.*

11. Socrates may feel that this citation is necessary because the story of the wealth of an entire region being spent on the wardrobe of only one woman, even the wife of the Great King, seems beyond probability.

12. As we have seen, he tries to stick to his claim that he could learn serious things from the many at 110e and following. Compare his attempts to maintain the position that there can be *philia* in the polis only because each does his own things at 127b and following.

13. This institution is studied in detail in Kenneth Dover, *Greek Homosexuality* (Cambridge, Mass.: Harvard University Press, 1989).

14. See Mark Munn, *The School of History: Athens in the Age of Socrates* (Berkeley: University of California Press, 2003), chapter 1.

15. See Eric Csapo for an account of the agonism of the pederastic relationship in Classical Athens and in particular of what was at stake for the boy beloved in this relationship ("Deep Ambivalence: Notes on a Greek Cockfight [Part I]," *Phoenix* 47, no. 1 [Spring 1993]: especially 18–28). Victoria Wohl takes up similar themes in an analysis of Alcibiades in Thucydides's *History of the Peloponnesian War* ("The Eros of Alcibiades," *Classical Antiquity* 18, no. 2 [October 1999]: 349–85); Wohl notes, 353–56, that Alcibiades is essentially, in Athenian terms, perverse, so that he serves both to reaffirm norms and to displace them through the desire he inspires in others. The author of the *Alcibiades* I seems to me to pick up on this perverse ambivalence in the Alcibiades and the Socrates of this dialogue. Compare David M. Halperin, who examines how the standard Athenian pederastic relationship was "socially and psychologically asymmetrical" ("Plato and Erotic Reciprocity," *Classical Antiquity* 5, no. 1 [April 1986]: 65–66).

16. Compare Socrates's parallel refusal to act "normally" at his trial by displaying his poor young children, his grieving friends, and the like (*Apology* 34b–e).

17. Some moves in this conversation are almost hair-raising in their fallaciousness. For example, 129d, when Alcibiades agrees that when a shoemaker cuts he cuts with his tools and with his hands.

18. See, for example, Mark Golden, *Children and Childhood in Classical Athens* (Baltimore: Johns Hopkins University Press, 1990), especially 23–50.

19. Alcibiades's remark at 121a that his family traces itself back to Eurysakes and through him to Zeus resonates with Alcibiades's war orphan status. Eurysakes was a king of Salamis and the son of Telamonian Ajax, who fought at Troy. Ajax did not return home, because he killed himself, leaving his infant son, the ancestor Alcibiades chooses to name, an orphan.

20. Isocrates, *On the Peace,* 82; Aeschines, *Against Ctesiphon,* 154. See Simon Goldhill for a discussion of a variety of ways, including the display of war orphans in the theater of Dionysus, in which democratic Athens impressed upon Athenians just how the polis should replace the household ("The Great Dionysia and Civic Ideology," *Journal of Hellenic Studies* 107 [1987]: 58–76).

21. Halperin argues with reference to the *Symposium* that Plato there borrows from and transforms the Athenian terms for describing pederasty to capture "the erotic, and aggressive, nature" of Socrates's practice of philosophy ("Erotic Reciprocity," 71–75). It seems to me that we see something similar to what Halperin sees in *Symposium* going on in *Alcibiades* I.

22. Socrates's conversation with Alcibiades is peppered with remarks that express a certain dismissive attitude toward the household (for example, the reference to a worthless nurse at 121d and the discussion of how there is no *philia* between husband and wife at 126e–27b), so it may be that he is proposing an erotic commitment *in opposition to* or alienated from the household. Likewise, his assurance that he will assist Alcibiades to achieve political success of a very particular kind in Athens, given his criticisms of politics in Athens, is proposing an alienation of Alcibiades from actual Athenian political life.

Chapter 2

1. For the fragments of Sappho, I use David Campbell's text in *Greek Lyric*, vol. 1 (Cambridge, Mass.: Harvard University Press, 1982). All translations are my own.

2. For example, Hesiod describes erõs as "the limb-loosener (*lusimelēs*) who subdues the mind and sensible counsel in the breasts of all gods and all humans" (*Theogony*, 120–22).

3. I consider my hermeneutical approach here to be essentially in line with that advocated by John Russon in "Hermeneutics and Plato's *Ion*," *Clio* 24 (1995): 399–418.

4. *Iliad*, 5.155, 11.342=20.412, 18.113=19.66, and so on.

5. I do not include here the remaining lines of the fragment, which are too lacunose to be analyzed effectively.

6. See Lewis Richard Farnell for a discussion of the mythic and cultic relationship of Aphrodite and divinities of the sea (*The Cults of the Greek States*, vol. 2 [Oxford: Clarendon Press, 1896], 636 and following).

7. These lines closely resemble lines from Sappho's fragment 1, the prayer to Aphrodite. In fragment 1, after Sappho has made her initial request to the god for her presence next to Sappho, the goddess appears and speaks, assuming that she knows what it is that Sappho wants from her. At lines 17 and 26–27, Aphrodite asks what it is that Sappho wants in her spirit to be accomplished.

8. Compare Polemarchus's definition of justice in *Republic* 1.

9. The word *emmoron* has been proposed as a textual supplement. The phrase *emmoron timas* is a tag from the *Odyssey* (8.480), used by Alcinous to describe singers. Given the frequency with which Sappho uses epic language, the suggestion appears highly likely.

10. *Odyssey* 8.63–64 states that Demodocus in particular was loved by the Muse, who took his sight but gave him divine voice as well.

11. Compare fragment 32, "who made me honoured (*timian*) by giving their own works/deeds (*erga*)."

12. Poems 98, 96, 129, 105, 47, 54, 58, and 59 likewise address issues of reciprocity and care.

13. This fragment continues for several more lines, but my concern is only with those I have quoted above.

14. This fragment begins with at least the second line of the poem, as is evident from the meter, two glyconics (lines 1 and 2 of each stanza) followed by a dactylic expansion (line 3 of the stanza); further, the first line of our fragment contains the connective particle *de*, which indicates almost always that the phrase or clause containing the *de* follows an earlier clause or phrase, which suggests that we begin after the beginning of "her" speech. It is not clear how much of the beginning of the poem is lost, so that it is not clear to what precise content Sappho's speech here is responding.

15. The use of the imperfect tense in Sappho's speech may also be insisting that the experience of the fair was more usual or habitual than the experience of the terrible, given

the imperfect tense's general use in descriptions of repeated or habitual action in the past. At the same time, Sappho as poet is using a fairly typical Archaic Greek poetic device, the use of antithesis to express completeness; *a* and *opposite-of-a* implies everything that falls in between *a* and *opposite-of-a*.

16. Anne Burnett notes that these lines stress the power of mind over experience: an experience of pain, remembered properly, can become a memory of beauty and pleasure ("Desire and Memory [Sappho Frag. 94]," *Classical Philology* 74, no. 1 [January 1979]: 18). Burnett points out that Sappho then goes on, in the lines that I do not include here, to remember an experience of beauty and pleasure.

17. See Egbert J. Bakker, "Storytelling in the Future: Truth, Time, and Tense in Homeric Epic," in *Written Voices: Spoken Signs,* ed. Bakker and Ahuvia Kahane (Cambridge, Mass.: Harvard University Press, 1997), 11–36.

18. Burnett notes that, in fragment 94, the memory of the past includes festal activity in honor of a god and that the "schema of experience" through memory that Sappho teaches her beloved here will culminate in the young woman's going on to relive her past with Sappho through more festal activity ("Desire and Memory," 23–25). I take up the question of festal activity and Sappho below.

19. On the identification of the roses of Pieria and the Muses, see Alex Hardie, "Sappho, the Muses, and Life After Death," *Zeitschrift für Papyrologie und Epigraphie* 154 (2005): 13, 31–32.

20. Epic *kleos* is the central theme throughout Gregory Nagy, *The Best of the Achaians: Concepts of the Hero in Archaic Greek Poetry,* rev. ed. (Baltimore: Johns Hopkins University Press, 1999). Hardie, in "Sappho, the Muses, and Life after Death," argues that in this poem Sappho condemns the addressee to anonymity through not using her name and, further, asserts her own claim to life after death through her association with the flowers of the Muses. Hardie notes that, in fact, Sappho was worshiped as a polis-hero in Mytilene (her home city) from the late fifth century onward (22). Hardie also notes that the Muses and flowers were regularly associated with mystery cults promising some version of life after death (31–32); Sappho is, on Hardie's view, likely taking advantage of that association in her poems.

21. One could here compare Rainer Maria Rilke's expression (in "Archaic Torso of Apollo") of the imperative inherent to truly witnessing to a work of art: "You must change your life."

22. Compare fragment 160, "these pleasures now for my / companions (*hetairais tais emais*) I shall sing beautifully." Sappho's song is something that she shares with her group. For the historical Sappho as a symposiast and leader of group festivities through a *thiasos* (ritual group), see Holt N. Parker, "Sappho Schoolmistress," *Transactions and Proceedings of the American Philological Association* 123 (1993): 309–51. A revision of Parker's argument appears in André Lardinois, "Subject and Circumstance in Sappho's Poetry," *Transactions and Proceedings of the American Philological Association* 124 (1994): 57–84.

23. Compare Jacques Derrida's argument for the necessary iterability of language in "Signature, Event, Context," in *Margins: Of Philosophy,* trans. Alan Bass (Chicago: University of Chicago Press, 1985), 307–31.

24. F. C. White argues this point at some length in "Love and Beauty in Plato's *Symposium,*" *Journal of Hellenic Studies* 109 (1989): 149–57.

25. E. E. Pender notes that Diotima's account of "spiritual pregnancy" works itself out as a desire for the same that would play on and appeal to the homoerotic ethos of the

participants at Agathon's symposium; Pender argues that, throughout Diotima's account of pregnancy, features peculiar to female pregnancy are suppressed ("Spiritual Pregnancy in Plato's *Symposium*," *Classical Quarterly* 42, no. 1 [1992]: 79–80).

26. The account of mortal participation in immortality that Diotima has so far offered is a pretty standard one. Compare, for example, the Homeric Hymn to Aphrodite (dated to the second half of the seventh century), which lays out the various ways in which human beings can participate in immortality: through sexual reproduction, through the founding of institutions, through the glory of song, and through grants of immortality to particular humans by the gods.

27. "For it they are willing to run risks and spend money and toil all sorts of toils and die for something." The *philotimia* that Diotima describes here is essentially the archaic mythic-heroic ethos best embodied by Achilleus (one of Diotima's own examples of *philotimia*), who chooses to die young in battle and thereby earn glory over living to a prosperous old age and having no glory. Each of Diotima's examples of *philotimia* (Alcestis, Achilleus, and Codrus) in fact comes from myth.

28. Compare the Muses' address to Hesiod and the other shepherds as bellies only (*gasteres oion*) at *Theogony* 26, or Odysseus's noting the force of the belly in driving people to perform dishonorable deeds at *Odyssey* 17.473–74, 18.53–54.

29. Gregory Vlastos sees in this account of eros an essentially self-centered love in which the beloved is lovable to the lover only as the means toward the lover's self-fulfillment (*Platonic Studies*, 2nd ed. [Princeton, N.J.: Princeton University Press, 1981], 3–34). Luce Irigaray seems to hold a similar view ("Sorcerer Love: A Reading of Plato's Symposium, Diotima's Speech," trans. Eleanor H. Kuykendall, *Hypatia* 3, no. 3 [Winter 1989]: 32–44), arguing (40–44) that Diotima's account of the lover seeking the beautiful itself is teleological and not functional, as Diotima's earlier account of love as bringing forth in the beautiful is. My point as the argument continues will be in part that self-fulfillment through the erotic relationship occurs for both lover and beloved and that this self-fulfillment, in philosophical lovers, also becomes the fulfillment of the community. See also D. C. Schindler, who argues that desire itself is at root self-centered, but Socrates's and Diotima's account of eros portrays it as self-transcending ("Plato and the Problem of Love: On the Nature of Eros in the 'Symposium,'" *Apeiron* 40, no. 3 [2007], especially 200–202).

30. Halperin ("Erotic Reciprocity") draws out the mutual dependence of lover and beloved in *Symposium* in a different way than I do here, focusing more on the desire of lover and beloved for each other. Nonetheless, my analysis here is sympathetic to Halperin's.

31. Diotima's use of *ëitheos* (young unmarried man) to describe the lover suggests that the relationship between lover and beloved is a marriage—the first marriage for each—and so a rite of passage for both into adulthood. *Ëitheos* is often used as the equivalent for males of *parthenos* for females: an adolescent at the point of maturity and ready to be married.

32. Compare Socrates's account of how he cares for his fellow Athenians by trying to help them care about excellence at *Apology* 29c and following.

33. Schindler notes that the way that Socrates sets up his account of eros takes precisely this form: he begins by asking Agathon questions and then represents a conversation between himself and Diotima; Socrates does not represent himself as an authoritative speaker, but as one who responds to the speeches and ideas of others ("Plato and the Problem of Love," 204).

34. Compare Sappho fragments 5 and 96 on presence and memory.

35. This shared raising of offspring again makes the relationship of lover and beloved like a marriage.

36. See the account of *philia* in the discussion of Sappho above. Notice that the *koinōnia* and *philia* of lover and beloved are greater than those shared by people who produce children. The producers of children, I assume, are envisioned here as legitimately married men and women in the context of the household. Diotima presents here a version of the pederastic relationship similar to what Socrates offers us in *Alcibiades* I: the pederastic relationship supplants the household. Given the ways in which Diotima sets up this relationship as a *marriage*, the supplanting of the household becomes more pointed.

37. Compare Alcibiades's account of accepting Socrates as his lover at 217a–19d, especially 218d–19a.

38. It may be the case that Diotima's portrayal of lover and beloved at 209, which focuses quite strictly on the lover and his actions, does not quite do justice to the situation it describes; it notes that the lover educates the beloved without pursuing its own point about the lover *becoming* someone who can educate.

39. This aspect of the beauty of the *logoi* is worked out in Diotima's account of the education of the lover at 210c and following.

40. Compare Halperin ("Erotic Reciprocity," especially 74 and following) for a discussion of how philosophy, according to *Symposium*, necessarily begins in eros. My point here is that *Symposium* shows us that tradition as such also begins in eros.

41. Compare Diotima's account of learning at 207e–f. She describes learning as taking care (*meletan*) to put a new memory in place of the old one that departs because knowledge is constantly leaving us. In the same way, the *logoi* will depart if we do not take care to keep resuscitating them. See Mary P. Nichols, who argues that Diotima's account of eros shows how Socrates is, like eros, always in need of others, specifically of others with whom to have conversations ("Socrates' Contest with the Poets in Plato's *Symposium*," *Political Theory* 32, no. 2 [April 2004]: 186–206). Nichols argues, as I do, that the account of eros here shows how eros both requires and supports the life of the group.

42. Compare also, for example, Euripides, *Medea* 627–44, where the chorus sings of how love (*erōtes*) in excess brings no good and drives a person mad.

43. See Anne Carson (*Eros the Bittersweet: An Essay* [Princeton, N.J.: Princeton University Press, 1986], 118–20) for a thorough working-out of this point.

44. Ilja Leonard Pfeijffer argues that the opening foil for Helen's love for Paris, armies, ships, and so on, are part of a thematic continuity with the results of Helen's choice of Paris, the Trojan War ("Shifting Helen: An Interpretation of Sappho, Fragment 16 [Voigt]," *Classical Quarterly* N.S. 50, no. 1 [2000]: 1–6). By invoking the machines of war at the beginning, Sappho sets before us just what Helen despised next to Paris, the possibility of war and violent requital for her betrayal of family and home.

45. Irigaray notes Diotima's initial appeals to the effects of desire on animals, linking it to a notion of eros as a "mediator of Becoming" with no object besides becoming; the eros of animals marks eros's embeddedness in the now ("Sorcerer Love," 37–38).

46. Forms of *keimai* (I am set) are often used interchangeably with middle/passive forms of *tithēmi* (I set).

47. Diotima's description of the behavior of lovers here is reminiscent of Alcibiades's description of Socrates as being like the Sirens at 216a–b; Alcibiades says that he must plug his ears and pull himself away from Socrates because Socrates could, like the Sirens,

make Alcibiades stay by his side until he dies. Plato draws in these passages on a trad-itional mythic-poetic understanding of the Sirens as hostile to tradition. I address this aspect of the Sirens and Plato's use of them in Socrates's discussion of education in the purified city of *Republic* 3 in chapter 3.

48. In each of these stages, presumably, the lover continues to produce *logoi* relevant to the particular beauty he is admiring.

49. According to Walter Burkert (*Greek Religion*, trans. John Raffan [Cambridge, Mass.: Harvard University Press, 1985]) and Pausanias (*Description of Greece*), the Athen-ians acknowledged the role of desire in the formation of bonds between citizens within the polis, worshiping Aphrodite in her aspect Aphrodite Pandemos, Aphrodite of the Whole People, as an important state god. Aphrodite Pandemos is described in Pausanias's speech in *Symposium*.

50. Compare Schindler ("Plato and the Problem of Love," 208); Schindler argues here that Plato makes love present in the *Symposium* by having Socrates acknowledge, praise, and pursue love's object, beauty, thereby enacting for readers the process Diotima de-scribes. This enacting is a version of the bringing-into-the-now that I am describing here. Compare Nichols ("Socrates' Contest," 200–201), who notes that Socrates's speech cul-minates in an attempt to perpetuate its message, that eros properly involves teaching and creating immortal *logoi* and participates in keeping political communities alive.

Chapter 3

1. On the importance of education, not just in the *Republic*, but in Plato's thought in general, see C. D. C. Reeve, *Philosopher-Kings: The Argument of Plato's Republic* (Princeton, N.J.: Princeton University Press, 1998), 220–21, 259–60.

2. See Reeve, 188, who argues that, as *mousikē* and *gymnastikē* are both aimed at the soul, in particular the reasoning and the spirited parts of the soul, education in the new city should be aimed, following the analogy between the soul and the city, at the guard-ian class and the ruler class. Richard Lewis Nettleship argues that Plato's adoption of the traditional Greek two-fold education derives from Plato's seeing in this type of education a recognition of the two-fold nature of the human soul (*The Theory of Education in the Republic of Plato* [New York: Teachers College Press, 1968], 27–29); it comprises a philo-sophical part and a spirited part, which must be put into and kept in a proper balance.

3. I use here Alan Bloom's translation of the *Republic* (New York: Basic Books, 1991).

4. Zdravko Planinc argues for the *Odyssey*'s central role as intertext, provider of struc-ture, and foil for much of Plato's writing; Planinc's focus is the cosmological writing (*Plato Through Homer: Poetry and Philosophy in the Cosmological Dialogue* [Columbia: University of Missouri Press, 2003], 10 and following).

5. See Planinc (10–11), who argues that readers of Plato need to learn to see in his texts *allusion* as well as quotation, and allusion that is less patent than the type of easily recognized allusion we find, for example, elsewhere in *Republic* 3 (such as the allusions to the Hesiodic five races of human beings and succession myth).

6. In the *Republic* passage, the verb translated here as "give" is *parechēi*, which has the basic meaning "hand over."

7. Indeed, those who die listening to the Sirens are guaranteed never to receive proper funerary ritual.

8. See, for example, Donna C. Kurtz and John Boardman, *Greek Burial Customs* (Ithaca, N.Y.: Cornell University Press, 1971), 134 and following; Despoina Tsiafakis, "Life and

Death at the Hands of a Siren," *Studia Varia from the J. Paul Getty Museum,* ed. Marion True and Mary Louise Hart (Los Angeles: Getty Publications, 2001), 7–24.

9. James Adam notes that this passage describes the effects of music upon the soul as a kind of smelting of metal (*The Republic of Plato,* 2nd ed. [Cambridge: Cambridge University Press, 1963], *ad* 411b8).

10. *Odyssey,* 5.396; 8.522; 19.136, 204, 205, 206, 208, 264; *Iliad,* 3.176.

11. At *Odyssey* 8.522, Odysseus melts and weeps hearing the song of Demodocus in the court of the Phaeacians. In *Odyssey* 19, a disguised Odysseus speaks with Penelope; she tells him the story of her difficulties in Odysseus's absence, while he tells her false stories about himself. At 19.136, Penelope tells Odysseus that she has melted away her heart longing for Odysseus; at 204 and 208, Penelope melts and weeps listening to Odysseus tell his lying story.

The appearances of this verb at 5.396 and 19.205 and 206 are all in similes. (Only 5.396 is not obviously consistent with the use established elsewhere in the poem.) There the joy of Odysseus seeing Ithaca from the sea is compared to the joy of a family seeing a father, long being melted by sickness, recover. The appearances in Book 19 are both in a simile comparing Penelope's melting and weeping to the melting of snow on a mountaintop.

The one appearance of the verb in *Iliad* is at 3.176, where Helen, telling Priam about the great Greek warriors out on the battlefield, among them her brother-in-law Agamemnon, refers to herself as melting into tears as she thinks of the parents and the daughter she left behind in Sparta when she came to Troy with Paris. Here, too, we see the elements of storytelling and weeping in the context. Consistent also throughout all of the appearances in both *Iliad* and *Odyssey* is the motif of weeping for kin: father, husband, parents, child. I do not as yet see that Plato is making any use of that final element of the word's complex of meaning.

12. Plato's allusion to the Sirens of the *Odyssey* here should be relevant also for the Sirens that appear in the Tale of Er at *Republic* 10.617b–c; my concern here is with the discussion of song in Book 3, so I will not be addressing those later Sirens.

13. Claude Calame, *Les choeurs de jeunes filles en Grèce archaïque* (Rome: Edizioni dell' Ateneo e Bizzarri, 1977), 1: 52–167, especially 100–103, 140–43.

14. *Theogony,* 53–62, 79–93, 915–17.

15. Recall here the frequency with which heroes are identified by patronymics, particularly in epic: Odysseus son of Laertes, Agamemnon son of Atreus, Achilleus son of Peleus and grandson of Aeacus, and so on.

16. Because all those who hear the Sirens' song die on the beach of the Sirens' island, they cannot carry word of the Sirens away and thereby participate in the creation of a reputation for the Sirens. The Sirens' activity normally ensures that the Sirens remain outside of the world of reputation. That the Sirens come to be known at all is a mark of their failure to kill Odysseus. They are known to us as part of the glorious reputation of that hero.

17. Compare Eva Stehle (*Performance and Gender in Ancient Greece* [Princeton, N.J.: Princeton University Press, 1997], 95–97) on Sirens as unvalidated models for choral song in Pindar's *Partheneion* II (ed. Bruno Snell and Herwig Maehler), fragment 94b. Stehle notes also that the Sirens are generally marked as "unknowns" in Greek poetry by their being associated with the wild places at the ends of the earth, "far from civilization or Olympus."

18. 9.673, 10.544, and 11.430.

19. 9.673 and 10.544.

20. 10.87 and 555; 11.511; 14.42.

21. *Odyssey* 3.79, 202.

22. See Nagy on the *Odyssey*'s provision of its own version of Trojan War myth, distinct from the Iliadic version (*Best of the Achaeans,* 55–65); the Odyssean take on Troy myth stresses different themes and values different manifestations of heroic excellence.

23. This theme runs throughout Nagy, *Greek Mythology and Poetics* (Ithaca: Cornell University Press, 1992).

24. Socrates rejects this story on the basis of a fairly simple-minded approach to the interpretation of myth: myth as *exemplum* for human behavior. Compare *Euthyphro* 5e–6d, where Socrates not only refuses to allow Euthyphro to use this same myth as justification for his own behavior but also refuses to engage at all in this type of interpretation of myth; he instead insists that Euthyphro try to define "the pious" for him. That Socrates here in *Republic* 3 accepts and engages in this lazy approach to understanding something complex and difficult is already a good indication that the surface claims here are not altogether honest. Later, at 378d, Socrates alludes to a more sophisticated approach to interpreting myth, through *huponoia,* through "understanding the meaning beneath the surface" (378d). This approach likewise is rejected, on the ground that the young are not yet able to discern lessons that are not explicit; Euthyphro, in this argument, would then have the interpretative sophistication of a child. See Adam, *Republic of Plato, ad* 378d 24. See also Reeve, who notes that the poems that will be acceptable in the guardians' curriculum will be the old poems, bowdlerized to become as much like the truth as possible (*Philosopher-Kings,* 228). Part of my point in what follows is to argue that it is only the traditional tales, free of bowdlerizing, that tell the truth or reveal the truth in the myths Socrates relates; ignorance of those stories leads to superficial and to some extent incorrect understanding of those myths.

25. Nettleship argues that the omission of the succession myth from education derives from the fact that this story portrays, repeatedly, the violation of *aidōs,* respect toward one's *philoi,* here parents. The holding of children in common, Nettleship goes on, is in part designed to spread the *aidōs* toward parents throughout the entire city. Consequently, a myth displaying violations of *aidōs* is especially to be kept from the new education (*Theory of Education,* 39–40). Compare Samuel Scolnicov, who stresses the role of education in promoting, not family-derived *aidōs,* but more group-oriented *homonoia* (*Plato's Metaphysics of Education* [London: Routledge 1988], 101–2).

26. The decision to create a story to be told to the new citizens is, in part, an acknowledgment of the power of the group and of tradition to educate individuals outside of education more strictly conceived. See Nettleship (*Theory of Education,* 5–7) on this notion of the nurture of society in education. Compare Scolnicov (*Plato's Metaphysics,* 113) on the value of mythic literature in education in the *Republic:* it is educative as a means to develop opinion, not knowledge. This power of the group to educate is explored in the *Apology* in Socrates's discussion of his first accusers.

27. Adam (*Republic of Plato, ad* 414b 16 and following) and Bloom ("Interpretive Essay," *The Republic of Plato* [New York: Basic Books, 1991], 455 note 66) point out that the reference to a Phoenician something here nods to Cadmus, a hero from Phoenicia who sowed dragon's teeth to create earth-born warriors, which is the basic model for Socrates's first foundation myth. Bloom also suggests that "Phoenician something" may allude to Odysseus's narration of his adventures to the Phaeacians; this suggestion seems to me without strong basis. I will address Cadmus and the Spartoi below.

28. See Luc Brisson for a discussion of Plato's association of the purveying of trad-itional mythic material with poets like Homer and Hesiod (*Plato the Myth Maker,* trans. Gerard Naddaf [Chicago: University of Chicago Press, 2000], 40–42). Many scholars of course point to a solidification in Plato's dialogues of the use of the word *muthos* to mean what we now in academic circles refer to as "myth." My point here is to stress that, while this solidification may in fact be taking place, it has not yet completed itself and that we need to be careful not to equivocate when we speak of Platonic *muthoi* as myths. See, for example, Gerard Naddaf ("Translator's Introduction," in *Plato the Myth Maker*) and Adi Ophir (*Plato's Invisible Cities: Discourse and Power in the Republic* [Savage, Md.: Barnes and Noble, 1991], 13–14), for sensible, and, in Naddaf's case, extremely thorough and helpful discussions of this issue. Brisson (*Plato the Myth Maker,* 142 and following) provides a statistical analysis of the meanings of the word *muthos* in the Platonic corpus; I would quarrel with some of Brisson's interpretations of the meaning attributed to this word in various passages, but his statistics do demonstrate unequivocally that the word as Plato uses it cannot be understood simply or even most frequently to mean "myth."

29. Socrates and Glaucon here state one of the essential aspects that define a myth: it must be accepted and retold by an audience to become traditional. See Burkert for a basic analysis of what he, and I, take as the defining features of myth (*Structure and History in Greek Mythology and Ritual* [Berkeley: University of California Press, 1979], 1–2). Brisson likewise accepts this feature of human interaction as key to marking a tale as a myth and not merely a story (*Plato the Myth Maker,* 64–65).

30. Adam notes that the myths created here are to ensure, in part at least, the perma-nence of the city (*Republic of Plato, ad* 414b and following); Socrates stresses this point in Book 4 at 424b–e when he insists that the guardians must ensure that the basic content of education in the new city not be changed. Claudia Baracchi argues that Socrates's founda-tion myths are also designed to discourage change within the citizens, and thereby in the city, by serving, through the myth of the metals, to remind people that they are what they are by nature and that change is not open to them; they must, as Baracchi says, "persist" (*Of Myth, Life and War in Plato's Republic* [Bloomington: Indiana University Press, 2002], 71–73). Compare my discussion of tradition and a living future above. Socrates's basic ap-proach to the mythic material is in fact a very traditional one: the tales exist to be retold in ways that serve the goals or interests of the teller. This stance toward myth on the part of the Greeks accounts for the fact that Homeric epic, produced during the eighth cen-tury, stresses the unproblematic unity of the aristocratic family, while tragedy, produced in democratic Athens in the fifth century, stresses the self-destructiveness of the aristocratic family and the curative strength of city-based institutions. The same basic story can be used in equally "traditional" ways to express radically different views.

31. This recycling of traditional material can of course be compared to the Sirens' offer to sing *some version* of the *Iliad* to Odysseus. Adam notes that the many points of similar-ity between Socrates's new myths and traditional Greek myth are the main reason that these stories will be, as Glaucon notes, believable over time (*Republic of Plato, ad* 415d–21).

32. No thorough account of Cadmus and the Spartoi from the Archaic or Classical period remains; we have testimony in a scholion to *Iliad* 2.494 that both Pherecydes and Hellanicus told this story. Apollonius of Rhodes (*Argonautica,* 3.1175 and following) also mentions it. For the episode involving Jason and sown men, Apollonius of Rhodes is our earliest elaborator (3.1278–1407); Pherecydes again is a source for this story, as is the fragmentary *Colchides* of Sophocles.

33. Reeve argues that this myth is an example of a useful lie that lies in words, while directing the soul toward the good or toward a truth; that truth here is the nurturing of the bonds of love and friendship that will tie the citizens of Callipolis together. These ties will be present already, Reeve contends, because of the mutual self-interest that was the founding principle of the original new city (*Philosopher-Kings*, 208–11). Brisson argues, along similar lines, that this myth accounts for the close bonds of citizens within the new city and for the features that naturally set those citizens apart (*Plato the Myth Maker*, 118–19).

34. The myths of Thebes, particularly as they were told by Athenian poets, portray the Theban royal family, descendants of Cadmus and the Spartoi, as self-destructive. The Theban royal family includes such figures as Dionysus, who causes the death of his cousin Pentheus at the hands of Pentheus's mother, Agave (as portrayed, for example, in Euripides's *Bacchae*), and Oedipus, who kills his father Laeus and pollutes his descendants with the taint of incest through his marriage to his mother Jocasta (as seen in Sophocles's *Antigone* or *Oedipus Tyrannus*).

35. Compare Ophir, who notes that, in this institution of new myth, the city will be taking over the memory of individual citizens, instilling a forgetfulness of these citizens as having a past with which they are continuous (*Plato's Invisible Cities*, 93). This discontinuity is, of course, essential to the transfer of allegiance from kin to city.

36. This displacement of *philia* from family to city-state is of course the prime plank of Classical Athenian democratic ideology. The official demands of the city-state do not, however, express the views of Athenian citizens about this contentious issue; resistance to the city-state's demand to rank kin lower than fellow-citizens is a major factor in Athens's continuous and aggressive propagation of her ideology throughout the fifth century. See, for example, Sophocles's *Antigone*, in which the competing demands of kin and city-state are worked out over the burial of Oedipus's son, Polyneices, with the demands of kin ultimately portrayed as more legitimate than those of the city-state. See Ophir, who discusses this passage in terms of its goal of blurring the distinction between the natural and the political (*Plato's Invisible Cities*, 96).

37. Compare Émile Benveniste on *philia* as based on recognition of certain others as "one's own"; this type of recognition of one's *philoi*, Benveniste argues, is the presupposition for attitudes of respect, concern, and defensive action (*Le vocabulaire des institutions indo-européennes* [Paris: Gallimard, 1969], 340–41).

38. The problematic nature of the rejection of kin-*philia* becomes more apparent if we accept Nettleship's argument that the key reason for the rejection of Hesiod's *Theogony* is its portrayal of the violation of *aidōs* toward parents (*Theory of Education*, 39–40). If one goal of education is to promote kin-*philia* among the citizens, how can that education function when we reject, outside of education, kin-*philia*?

39. As Socrates himself admits at 8.546a–b, when he introduces the issue of the inevitable decay of things. Diskin Clay argues that Adeimantus's remark at 4.421c that Socrates's guardians will not be personally happy is an indication on Plato's part that his readers should carefully evaluate the arguments put forward throughout the *Republic* ("Reading the *Republic*," in *Platonic Writings, Platonic Readings*, ed. C. L. Griswold, Jr. [University Park: Pennsylvania State University Press, 2002], 22). My point here is that, in his account of the function of musical education, Plato's use of allusion serves much the same function: to warn us that we should not simply take Socrates's arguments and claims at face value. Compare Baracchi, *Of Myth, Life and War*, 3, who notes that the text of the *Republic* gives itself as a task that we must accomplish through careful and flexible reading. See also

Planinc, *Plato Through Homer,* 13, who argues that we must be prepared to see the Platonic text refigured as we come to understand it more fully.

40. See, for example, Pseudo-Xenophon, *Constitution of the Lacedaemonians,* for a précis of the major points in the elite Spartan way of life.

41. See, for example, the two collections in Plutarch's *Moralia, Sayings of Spartans* and *Sayings of Spartan Women;* each collection contains material dating from the fourth century B.C.E. (Plato's century) to Plutarch's own period (mid-first to second century C.E.) that expresses what were regarded by other Greeks as the most excellent aspects of the Spartan character.

42. Socrates's reference to *Phoinikikon ti,* a certain Phoenician thing, at 414c serves to direct us to focus on the earth-born as part of the Cadmus myth, since Cadmus came to Greece from Phoenicia in search of his sister Europa.

43. *Sayings of Spartan Women* in particular stresses the emotional commitment of elite women to the city before their blood-kin; for example, the story of Damatria, who is said to have killed her son, who had himself deserted in war (*Sayings of Spartan Women* 240f). The *Sayings* also mentions a woman who, upon hearing that her son had survived a battle and escaped capture by the enemy, wrote a letter to her son advising him that, as he now had a bad reputation, he should eradicate that reputation or die (241d).

44. For example, legislation designed to encourage Spartiatae to marry and produce multiple offspring was introduced. The Spartans wish to strike a truce to retrieve the one hundred twenty Spartiatae besieged by the Athenians at Sphacteria in 425 (Thucydides, *History,* 4.38–39); roughly sixty years earlier, the few Spartiatae who survived the battle of Thermopylae were shamed by their fellow citizens (see Herodotus, *Histories,* 7.229–32, for the stories of Aristodemus and Pantites). See G. L. Cawkwell, "The Decline of Sparta," *Classical Quarterly* N.S. 33, no. 2 (1983): 385–95.

45. Paul Cartledge, *Sparta and Lakonia: A Regional History 1300–362 BC,* 2nd ed. (London: Routledge, 2002), 271.

46. Simon Hornblower, *The Greek World 479–323 BC,* 4th ed. (London: Routledge, 2011), 181 and following.

47. Cartledge, 234–36.

48. Cartledge, 263–72.

Chapter 4

1. All translations of the *Laws* come from *The Laws of Plato,* trans. Thomas L. Pangle (Chicago: University of Chicago Press, 1980).

2. See Nicholas F. Jones ("The Organization of the Kretan City in Plato's *Laws,*" *Classical World* 83, no. 6 [July–August 1990]: 473–92). Jones notes (475) that the new city is a reconstruction on an old site, a fact that points to the *politeia* constructed in *Laws* being a reconstruction of the cities upon whose laws the laws of the new city are based.

3. See Glenn R. Morrow (*Plato's Cretan City: A Historical Interpretation of the Laws* [Princeton, N.J.: Princeton University Press, 1960]). Morrow (96–97) sees the criticism of naval warfare here as a manifestation of late fifth- and early fourth-century criticism of Pericles's strategy for the conduct of the Peloponnesian War (to avoid infantry battle with the Spartans by abandoning the agricultural territory of Attica to the Spartans and to withdraw into the walls of the city, fighting primarily by ship), which troubled many Athenians because this policy manifested "unwillingness to preserve the sacred soil of Attica." Inherent in this criticism is Athenian reverence for and attachment to their land,

their territory. Compare Jim Roy ("The Threat from Piraeus," in *Kosmos: Essays in Order, Conflict and Community,* ed. Paul Cartledge, Paul Millet, and Sitta von Reden [Cambridge: Cambridge University Press, 1998], 191–202). At 191–200, Roy locates the discussion at *Laws* 4.704a–07d within an Athenian debate about the Peiraieus (the main commercial port of Athens) as a location that undermined the Athenian citizen body because it provided a place for groups of Athenians to engage in bad behavior, such as prostitution and dishonest business practices. Morrow and Roy both point to Athenian discomfort with Athens's reliance on its navy and ports and the opposition between Athens proper (including her sacred soil) and those parts of the polis associated with the navy.

4. All translations of the *Odyssey* are my own. Jones notes ("Kretan City," 492) that the *politeia* constructed by the Athenian Stranger promotes the introversion of the demes, in particular, through their being coherently internally organized and kept out of the work of government. This isolation and internal coherence are parallel to the isolation and internal lawgiving coherence of the households of the Cyclopes.

5. Compare Hesiod's account of the coming end of the Iron Age at *Works and Days* 174–201: there will be no agreement among people, no respect for oaths, but violence and praise for violence; here violence is the result of a general and radical idiosyncrasy.

6. The passage in *Laws* 4 under discussion here is, of course, very much concerned with ships as providing contact with other cities and peoples. Given that many of the new settlers are supposed to come from mainland Greece, in particular the Peloponnese (708a), the role of ships in city-foundation is also relevant to *Laws* 4.

7. Compare Erwin F. Cook (*The Odyssey at Athens: Myths of Cultural Origins* [Ithaca, N.Y.: Cornell University Press, 1995]). Cook argues (97–100) that the *Odyssey* marks the Cyclopes as being without the social laws associated with the agora, the site of counsel and "corporate political memory." He notes, further, that their living, essentially, in a paradise in which everything they need comes spontaneously from the earth is what causes their excessive violence, their *hybris.*

8. Cook remarks on the association in the account of Polyphemus and the Cyclopes of ships, commerce, and *culture* as lined up against the Cyclopes (*Odyssey at Athens,* 108–9).

9. The poem indicates that this attack is not part of any plan of warfare, but is simple opportunism, when it says, "carrying me from Ilium the wind brought me near the Cicones at Ismarus" (*Odyssey* 9.39–40).

10. Odysseus's transition from simple violent exploiter to guest of course depends also on his increasing vulnerability before those he meets: over the course of his wanderings he loses all of his companions. To understand himself as vulnerable, open to the wills of others, is to cease to see the world as for himself.

11. Compare the theme of authoritative poetry that we studied in chapter 3.

12. Compare Plutarch's account of Lycurgus's introduction of his constitution to Sparta in chapter 5 of his *Life* of Lycurgus. Lycurgus wins over supporters secretly and then, with thirty armed elite men, occupies the Spartan agora—his reforms come as part of a coup. He then announces his new *politeia,* claiming that it was given to him by Pythian Apollo.

13. See, for example, Book 1, 645c—a city should take over a *logos* from the gods and set that *logos* as a law for itself. Compare Book 4, 715e and following—the god holds the beginning (*archēn*) and end (*teleutēn*) and the middle of all the things that are.

14. See Thomas L. Pangle ("The Political Psychology of Religion in Plato's *Laws,*" *American Political Science Review* 70, no. 4 [December 1976]: 1059–77). Pangle's discussion here focuses on *Laws* 10 and the arguments there about theology and the nature of

the soul. His point (1059) is that all the laws the Athenian proposes are "proposed with an eye to the god at all times." He notes further (1060) that a healthy political life, for Plato, must include myth and religion. My point here is that the god is central to the idea of the *politeia* already in Book 1.

15. That is, the response can be a rejection similar to the fear of the strange encouraged by isolation.

16. Compare John Russon, "Heidegger, Hegel, and Ethnicity: The Ritual Basis of Self-Identity," *Southern Journal of Philosophy* 33, no. 4 (Winter 1995): 509–32.

17. Megillus's response to the rituals of other cities reminds us that the first generation of citizens in the new city will be in the same position as Megillus with respect, not just to ritual within the new city, but to all its institutions. They will be people who grew up under other laws. Compare Morrow, who notes that a major project of the new *politeia* articulated in *Laws* is to "harmonize" laws drawn from a variety of cities to create a single homogeneous citizen body out of settlers from several different cities (*Cretan City,* 547). Jones remarks on the same point: he sees the primary problem of the new foundation to be overcoming the "rootlessness and disunity" of a new city whose settlers come from multiple cities ("Kretan City," 473–75).

18. See Calame, *Les choeurs de jeunes filles en Grèce archaïque,* 100–103, 140–43.

19. See Burkert, *Greek Religion,* 146–47.

20. Compare the choral entry-song in Euripides's *Bacchae* (64–167), in which the chorus of Lydian maenads describes the god participating, as celebrant, in the rituals in his honor.

21. Marcel Detienne notes that the drinking of unmixed wine by the old men in the new city has wine in Dionysiac ritual take the place of *mania* in Dionysiac myth (*Dionysus at Large,* trans. Arthur Goldhammer [Cambridge, Mass.: Harvard University Press, 1989], 23).

22. This Lycurgus is not the lawgiver of Laconia, but a king, son of Dryas, in Asia Minor.

23. According to *Iliad* 6.130–40, Zeus grows angry at Lycurgus and blinds him. Apollodoros, *Bibliotheca,* 3.5.1 tells us that Lycurgus, mad, kills his own son, Dryas, with an ax, thinking that he is cutting vines; the people of his city then, on the orders of Dionysus, kill Lycurgus.

24. Other versions of this pattern include the myth of the daughters of Minyas and the myth of Dionysus's introduction of wine to Attica through the mediation of the farmer, Icarius.

25. See Detienne, who notes that Dionysus-myth consistently portrays the god introducing his own worship to humans in his role as the Stranger; these myths insist, Detienne argues, on violence and defilement (brought on by the god's imposition of madness) followed by purification (achieved through accepting the god) (*Dionysus at Large,* 23).

26. See Richard Seaford, "Dionysus as Destroyer of the Household: Homer, Tragedy, and the Polis," in *Masks of Dionysus,* eds. Thomas H. Carpenter and Christopher A. Faraone (Ithaca, N.Y.: Cornell University Press, 1993), 115–46. Seaford argues here that Dionysus is the divine opponent of a tendency on the part of the city and especially of the household toward a false sense of self-sufficiency, manifested mythically, for example, as the endogamy of incest in Sophocles's *Oedipus Tyrannus* (see especially 138–41).

27. Compare the potential of the new foundation here to the situation of isolated and conservative Sparta in the fourth century, discussed in chapter 3 above.

28. It will be apparent from my arguments here that I disagree with Andrea Nightingale, who argues (in many regards compellingly) that *Laws,* through the way it is written, provides no discursive strategy to challenge or undermine the authority of the Stranger as lawgiver ("A Literary Interpretation of Plato's *Laws,*" *Classical Philology* 88, no. 4 [October 1993]: 279–300). In my view, through the inclusion of mythic material, Plato precisely opens up the Stranger's authority to question. This chapter is a revised version of my paper "'He Saw the Cities and He Knew the Minds of Many Men': Landscape and Character in the *Odyssey* and the *Laws,*" in *Plato's Laws: Force and Truth in Politics,* eds. Gregory Recco and Eric Sanday (Bloomington: Indiana University Press, 2013), 105–17.

Chapter 5

1. This formulation derives from Burkert, *Structure and History in Greek Mythology and Ritual,* 1, 22–29.

2. Oedipus thus undergoes a transformation not uncommon in Athenian tragedy: a murderer from elsewhere is taken in by Athens and becomes a source of good for the city. We see this movement with Orestes in Aeschylus's *Eumenides* and Heracles in Euripides's *Heracles,* for example.

3. Xenophon, in his *Apology,* mentions Chairephon's consulting the oracle of Apollo about Socrates, but his Socrates never mentions any testing of the oracle. Plato's language is specific in constructing an Oedipus-like Socrates. On the Socrates of the *Apology* as a constructed image of Socrates, see Bernard Freydberg, "Retracing Homer and Aristophanes in the Platonic Text," in *Retracing the Platonic Text,* ed. John Russon and John Sallis (Evanston, Ill.: Northwestern University Press, 2000), 99–112.

4. Sophocles's use of these words in *Oedipus Tyrannus* is marked. The noun *elenchos* and the verb *elenchō* appear three times *in toto* in the play (333, 603, and 783); in each of these appearances the word is applied to Oedipus's behavior and stance. The verb *zēteō* and the noun *zētēma* appear seven times (110, 266, 278, 362, 450, 659, and 1112); all but one of these uses (that at 659) refer to Oedipus's investigation regarding Laius's murder. Plato's text exploits the charged character of these words.

5. Socrates goes on at 22a7–8 to say that he continued with his labors so that the oracle would turn out to be irrefutable—*anelenktos;* in that case, Socrates is now doing the *opposite* of what he started to do. But he immediately says that he next went to question the poets on the assumption that among these men he would find someone wiser than himself. The sense of the context seems to demand that Socrates at 22a7–8 be saying that he continues with his labors so that the oracle *not* prove irrefutable. Burnett does not find a problem here, but some editors have inserted a *mē* into this clause. At any rate, because there seems to be some controversy over the correct reading at this point, I am not basing anything on the presence of *anelenktos* here.

6. Herodotus, *Histories,* 1.53.

7. The Greek word that normally designates the labors of Heracles is *athlos,* contest or struggle. Related to *athlos,* contest, is *athlon,* prize. In mythic literature, the idea of the prize is essentially an aristocratic idea; noble men, heroes, compete with other heroes for the visible signs of their excellence. This ethos also permeates the world of ancient athletic competition, which was exclusively aristocratic in its self-presentation and which held Heracles up as the athlete par excellence. Accepting that this passage in the *Apology* is alluding to Heracles's labors, I wonder if Plato is in some way "democratizing" the aristocratic notion of the heroic struggle here to suit his Socrates by replacing the highly

evocative *athlos* with *ponos*. This overturning of the aristocratic ethos may also be at play in Socrates's suggestion that the penalty he pay for his conviction be being served meals at public expense in the prytaneum, a reward which, he notes, is generally given to victors at the pan-Hellenic athletic competitions (36d–e). I will have more to say on a related question in the final section of this chapter.

8. At 232, 335, 342, 364, 385, 461, 509 (both words), 1022, 1358, 1412, and 1674.

9. See, for example, Pausanias, 1.28.7; 1.30.4. At 1.28.7, Pausanias says that Oedipus's bones were brought from Thebes and given a tomb in the precinct of the Furies.

10. Again at 31a–b, Socrates says the he has been given (*dedosthai*) by the god to the city.

11. Forms of *oida/eidenai*—to know—appear six times in *Apology* 21d.

12. The exceptions are Orpheus and Musaeus, both mythic poets, mention of whom the Homeric poems would avoid because these poets are exemplars of rival traditions.

13. For example, *Iliad* 2.860, 874; 9.184, 191.

14. Odysseus *does* speak with the shade of his companion Elpenor without Elpenor having tasted the mixture. In this case, consciousness is a sign of the dead Elpenor's liminal status, as he has not been fully absorbed among the dead because his corpse is still unburied (11.51–54).

15. Some resemblance to Teiresias may appear in the gift-curse theme as well. Teiresias is commonly said to have earned his prophetic gifts as compensation for his being struck blind by one of the gods, usually Hera or Athene (Pindar, *Nemean*, 1.91; Callimachus, *Hymn* 5 ["The Baths of Pallas"]; Ovid, *Metamorphoses*, 3.316–38, for example).

16. When I refer to "democracy" and "democratic" in this chapter, I mean very particularly fifth-century Athenian democracy, not early twenty-first-century pluralistic democracy.

17. For detailed discussion of tragedy and democracy, see Richard Seaford, *Reciprocity and Ritual: Homer and Tragedy in the Developing City-State* (Oxford: Oxford University Press, 1994), and Jean-Pierre Vernant and Pierre Vidal-Naquet, *Myth and Tragedy in Ancient Greece,* trans. Janet Lloyd (New York: Zone Books, 1988).

18. Both Socrates and Oedipus follow the traditional pattern of the scapegoat: the community faces a situation of anxiety, a scapegoat is selected, rites of adornment or communication are performed that bring the scapegoat into contact with the entire community, the scapegoat is expelled from the community, the anxiety is relieved. It is also the case that the Athenians, litigious as they were under the democracy, only heard trials for impiety in situations of political anxiety. See Robert Parker, who cites the trials for impiety following the mutilation of the herms in 415 (*Athenian Religion: A History* [Oxford: Oxford University Press, 1996], 202). This act of impiety was regarded by the Athenians as part of a conspiracy against the democratic government. The city was particularly unsettled at this point because the Athenians were about to send the bulk of their fleet to Sicily, a controversial and daring decision. In 399, barely five years after Athens's final defeat in the Peloponnesian War, the city was still suffering from the social and economic effects of that war. Further, hostility against the Thirty Tyrants, the murderous oligarchic government installed by Sparta after the defeat, among whom several of Socrates's associates were found, remained bitter, despite the fact that the Thirty had been expelled in 403. Tensions with Sparta likewise continued.

19. For discussion of archaic epic and pan-Hellenic ideology, see Nagy, *Best of the Achaeans.*

20. We could see Plato's assimilation of Socrates to Oedipus as a critique of democratic Athens, as if it were saying, "We Athenians celebrate, honor, and rely on the repulsive

kin-killing foreign aristocrat Oedipus while we reject our own fellow-citizen, Socrates. Oedipus, of course, is dead and tamed through cult, so he cannot bother us, but Socrates alive makes us very uncomfortable."

21. Which was arguably still the dominant way of thinking and understanding in fifth- and fourth-century Athens. This chapter is a substantially revised version of my paper "Plato's Oedipus: Myth and Philosophy in the *Apology*," in *Reexamining Socrates in the "Apology*," Fagan and Russon, 85–101.

Chapter 6

1. In *Crito*, then, we see something quite similar to what we see in *Apology* with Socrates's likening himself to Oedipus: a Platonic reenactment of a traditional story.

2. On the nature of Odysseus's speech, see Michael Lynn-George, *Epos: Word, Narrative, and the Iliad* (Atlantic Highlands, N.J.: Humanities Press, 1988).

3. Phoenix is a member of the contingent Achilleus leads.

4. See Scott Kramer for a discussion of how Socrates's dream invites the interpretation that Socrates will be willing to escape to Thessaly and how that interpretation foreshadows the major theme of the dialogue, the choice of Socrates ("Socrates' Dream: *Crito* 44a–b," *Classical Journal* 83, no. 3 [February–March 1988]: 193–97).

5. Another striking parallel to the *Crito:* Is Socrates, like Agamemnon, reporting a false dream to Crito?

6. Compare the "old charges" against Socrates: *Apology* 18b.

7. See Nagy, "The Worst of the Achaeans," appendix to *Best of the Achaeans.*

8. Even Achilleus, who Thersites acknowledges is much better than Agamemnon at *Iliad* 2.239–40, does not escape Thersites's abuse here. Thersites says that Achilleus did not kill Agamemnon for the dishonor Agamemnon did to him because he was *methēmōn*, forgiving or relaxed or careless. The implication of that word is that Achilleus should have killed Agamemnon but did not.

9. Compare Socrates on the value of "taking a stand": *Apology* 28d.

10. Kramer notes that Crito, in proposing flight to Thessaly, reiterates the words of the beautiful woman in Socrates's dream ("Socrates' Dream," 196).

11. On the issue of images of Socrates, see Freydberg, "Retracing Homer and Aristophanes in the Platonic Text."

12. Compare Socrates's discussion of dying in *Apology*. There he says that he does not fear death because he has no idea what it will be to die. Dying could in fact turn out to be the greatest blessing (*Apology* 40c5–41b7).

13. Compare Mitchell Miller, who argues that Crito, an "Athenian Everyman," makes Socrates out to be someone who overturns proper values by harming his friends and helping his enemies ("'The Arguments I Seem to Hear': Argument and Irony in the *Crito*," *Phronesis* 41, no. 2 [1996]: 122–23).

14. Ruby Blondell notes that this passage in *Crito* makes the various aspects of Socratic self-consistency very clear. This consistency, she argues, lies at the root of the trust and reliability that make all human relationships possible (*The Play of Character in Plato's Dialogues* [Cambridge: Cambridge University Press, 2002], 117).

15. Miller notes that what Socrates is pointing out here is that Crito's behavior in *Crito* indicates that Crito never understood the *logoi* to which he agreed ("Arguments I Seem to Hear," 134). See also Thomas C. Brickhouse and Nicholas D. Smith, who lay out some of the ways in which both *Apology* and *Crito* assume and articulate some "axiomatic" Socratic

principles about justice and the soul, such as the notion that the soul is our most precious possession (*Socrates on Trial* [Princeton, N.J.: Princeton University Press, 1989], 156–59).

16. Roslyn Weiss notes that Socrates's conversation with the laws is aimed at convincing Crito that Socrates should not escape and at changing Crito's understanding of the issues at stake for Socrates, despite the fact that Socrates has the laws address him and not Crito, the one proposing flight from Athens (*Socrates Dissatisfied: An Analysis of Plato's Crito* [Oxford: Oxford University Press, 1998], 85, 118, 156–58).

17. See Gregory Recco for a more thorough working-out of this point (*Athens Victorious: Democracy in Plato's Republic* [Lanham, Md.: Rowman and Littlefield, 2008], 75). Recco notes, further, that an incorrect verdict on the part of any particular jury does not undermine the overall authority of the laws.

18. Compare the discussion of Oedipus's obedience to traditional authority in chapter 5.

19. See Recco, who discusses how Socrates's very ability to engage in philosophy is rooted in the laws of Athens (*Athens Victorious*, 82–85).

20. Weiss notes that, when the laws discuss the possibility of Socrates's going to Thessaly in particular, they stress that the lawlessness of Thessaly makes it a place particularly uncongenial to Socrates (*Socrates Dissatisfied*, 126–27). Compare Blondell, who notes that Plato's Socrates is inherently cosmopolitan in that his associates include many metics and foreigners, all of whom have come to Athens; Plato thereby makes Athens the center of the philosophical world (*Play of Character*, 78). That aspect of Athens is of course also at play in Socrates's rejection of Thessaly.

21. Blondell notes that we see in Socrates's account of his relationship to Athens in these passages a particularly clear manifestation of the way in which Plato has written Socrates as embedded in a very particular historical and cultural moment (democratic Athens in the late fifth century) (*Play of Character*, 75).

22. Weiss argues that this statement, which includes a comparison of Socrates to the Corybantes, ecstatic worshipers of the Great Mother, indicates that Socrates does not find the arguments he puts in the mouths of the laws in fact convincing (*Socrates Dissatisfied*, 137–40). I find Weiss's point intriguing but, as I have argued, I see Socrates expressing some fairly profound truths about himself, law, and tradition through his personified laws. Socrates's distancing himself from the laws' arguments may complicate those arguments but it does not fundamentally undermine them.

23. Some scholars take Crito's silence at this point as an indication that Crito has understood and to some extent taken up the points that Socrates has made. See, for example, Weiss, *Socrates Dissatisfied*, 134–41; Miller, "Arguments I Seem to Hear," 135–36. I find these discussions unconvincing because, as I indicate, I see no evidence that Socrates has done anything other than silence Crito.

Conclusion

1. Baracchi, *Of Myth, Life, and War*, and Recco, *Athens Victorious*, are important steps in this direction.

Adam, James. *The Republic of Plato.* 2nd ed. 2 vols. Cambridge: Cambridge University Press, 1963.

Aeschines. *Tragoediae.* Edited by Denys Page. Oxford: Clarendon Press, 1972.

Annas, Julia. *An Introduction to Plato's Republic.* Oxford: Oxford University Press, 1981.

Apollodoros. *The Library.* Translated by J. G. Frazer. Cambridge, Mass.: Harvard University Press, 1921.

Bakker, Egbert J. "Storytelling in the Future: Truth, Time, and Tense in Homeric Epic," in *Written Voices: Spoken Signs,* edited by Egbert J. Bakker and Ahuvia Kahane. Cambridge, Mass.: Harvard University Press, 1997, 11–36.

Baracchi, Claudia. *Of Myth, Life, and War in Plato's Republic.* Bloomington: Indiana University Press, 2002.

Benveniste, Émile. *Le vocabulaire des institutions indo-européennes.* Paris: Gallimard, 1969.

Blondell, Ruby. *The Play of Character in Plato's Dialogues.* Cambridge: Cambridge University Press, 2002.

Bloom, Alan. "Interpretive Essay," in *The Republic of Plato.* 2nd ed. Translated by Alan Bloom. New York: Basic Books, 1991, 305–436.

Bluck, R. S. "The Origin of the *Greater Alcibiades.*" *Classical Quarterly* N.S. 3, nos. 1–2 (1953): 46–52.

Brann, Eva. "The Music of the *Republic.*" *Agon* 1 (1967): 1–117.

Brickhouse, Thomas C., and Nicholas D. Smith. *Socrates on Trial.* Princeton, N.J.: Princeton University Press, 1989.

Brisson, Luc. *Plato the Myth Maker.* Translated by Gerard Naddaf. Chicago: University of Chicago Press, 2000.

Burkert, Walter. *Greek Religion.* Translated by John Raffan. Cambridge, Mass.: Harvard University Press, 1985.

Burkert, Walter. *Structure and History in Greek Mythology and Ritual.* Berkeley: University of California Press, 1979.

Burnett, Anne. "Desire and Memory (Sappho Frag. 94)." *Classical Philology* 74, no. 1 (January 1979): 16–27.

Calame, Claude. *Les choeurs de jeunes filles en Grèce archaïque.* 2 vols. Rome: Edizioni dell' Ateneo e Bizzarri, 1977.

Callimachus. *Hymns and Epigrams.* Translated by A. W. Mair and G. R. Mair. Cambridge, Mass.: Harvard University Press, 1921.

Campbell, David. *Greek Lyric.* Vol. 1. Cambridge, Mass.: Harvard University Press, 1982.

Carson, Anne. *Eros the Bittersweet: An Essay.* Princeton, N.J.: Princeton University Press, 1986.

Cartledge, Paul. *Sparta and Lakonia: A Regional History 1300–362 BC.* 2nd ed. London: Routledge, 2002.

Cawkwell, G. L. "The Decline of Sparta." *Classical Quarterly* N.S. 33, no. 2 (1983): 385–400.

Clark, Pamela M. "The *Greater Alcibiades.*" *Classical Quarterly* N.S. 5, nos. 3–4 (1955): 231–40

Clay, Diskin. "Reading the *Republic,*" in *Platonic Writings, Platonic Readings,* edited by C. L. Griswold, Jr. University Park: Pennsylvania State University Press, 2002, 19–33.

Cook, Erwin F. *The Odyssey at Athens: Myths of Cultural Origins.* Ithaca, N.Y.: Cornell University Press, 1995.

Csapo, Eric. "Deep Ambivalence: Notes on a Greek Cockfight (Part I)." *Phoenix* 47, no. 1 (Spring 1993): 1–28.

Denyer, Nicholas. *Plato: Alcibiades.* Cambridge: Cambridge University Press, 2001.

Derrida, Jacques. "Signature, Event, Context." In *Margins: Of Philosophy,* translated by Alan Bass. Chicago: University of Chicago Press, 1985, 307–31.

Detienne, Marcel. *Dionysus at Large.* Translated by Arthur Goldhammer. Cambridge, Mass.: Harvard University Press, 1989.

Dover, Kenneth. *Greek Homosexuality.* Cambridge, Mass.: Harvard University Press, 1989.

Euripides. *Fabulae,* 3 vols. Edited by James Diggle. Oxford: Clarendon Press, 1981–94.

Fagan, Patricia, and John Russon, eds. *Reexamining Socrates in the* "Apology." Evanston, Ill.: Northwestern University Press, 2009.

Farnell, Lewis Richard. *The Cults of the Greek States,* vol. 2. Oxford: Clarendon Press, 1896.

Faulkner, Andrew. *The Homeric Hymn to Aphrodite.* Oxford: Oxford University Press, 2008.

Foley, John Miles. *Immanent Art: From Structure to Meaning in Traditional Oral Epic.* Bloomington: Indiana University Press, 1991.

Freydberg, Bernard. "Retracing Homer and Aristophanes in the Platonic Text." In *Retracing the Platonic Text,* edited by John Russon and John Sallis, 99–112. Evanston, Ill.: Northwestern University Press, 2000.

Golden, Mark. *Children and Childhood in Classical Athens.* Baltimore: Johns Hopkins University Press, 1990.

Goldhill, Simon. "The Great Dionysia and Civic Ideology." *Journal of Hellenic Studies* 107 (1987): 58–76.

Gregory, George. "Of Socrates, Aristophanes, and Rumors." In Fagan and Russon, *Reexamining Socrates in the* "Apology," 35–61.

Hall, Edith. *Inventing the Barbarian: Greek Self-Definition Through Tragedy.* Oxford: Oxford University Press, 1989.

Halperin, David M. "Plato and Erotic Reciprocity." *Classical Antiquity* 5, no. 1 (April 1986): 60–80.

Halperin, David M. "Platonic *Eros* and What Men Call Love." *Ancient Philosophy* 5 (1985): 161–204.

Hardie, Alex. "Sappho, the Muses, and Life After Death." *Zeitschrift für Papyrologie und Epigraphie* 154 (2005): 13–32.

Harrison, Thomas. *The Emptiness of Asia: Aeschylus' Persians and the History of the Fifth Century.* London: Duckworth, 2000.

Herodotus. *The Histories.* Translated by Robin Waterfield. Oxford: Oxford University Press, 2008.

Hesiod. *Works and Days.* Edited by M. L. West. Oxford: Oxford University Press, 1982.

Hesiod. *Theogony.* Edited by M. L. West. Oxford: Oxford University Press, 1966.

Homer. *Opera.* 5 vols. Edited by D. B. Monro and W. T. Allen. Oxford: Oxford University Press, 1912–20.

Hornblower, Simon. *The Greek World 479–323 BC.* 4th ed. London: Routledge, 2011.

Irigaray, Luce. "Sorcerer Love: A Reading of Plato's Symposium, Diotima's Speech." Translated by Eleanor H. Kuykendall. *Hypatia* 3, no. 3 (Winter 1989): 32–44.

Isocrates. *Isocrates,* vol. 2. Translated by George Norlin. Cambridge, Mass.: Harvard University Press, 1929.

Jones, Nicholas F. "The Organization of the Kretan City in Plato's *Laws.*" *Classical World* 83, no. 6 (July–August 1990): 473–92.

Kosman, L. A. "Platonic Love," in *Facets of Plato's Philosophy,* edited by W. H. Werkmeister. Assen, Netherlands: Van Gorcum, 1976, 53–69.

Kramer, Scott. "Socrates' Dream: *Crito* 44a–b." *Classical Journal* 83, no. 3 (February–March 1988): 193–97.

Kurtz, Donna C., and John Boardman. *Greek Burial Customs.* Ithaca, N.Y.: Cornell University Press, 1971.

Labarbe, J. *L'Homère de Platon.* Paris: Les Belles Lettres, 1987.

Lardinois, André. "Subject and Circumstance in Sappho's Poetry." *Transactions and Proceedings of the American Philological Association* 124 (1994): 57–84.

Lynn-George, Michael. *Epos: Word, Narrative, and the Iliad.* Atlantic Highlands, N.J.: Humanities Press, 1988.

Miller, Margaret C. *Athens and Persia in the Fifth Century BC: A Study in Cultural Receptivity.* Cambridge: Cambridge University Press, 1997.

Miller, Mitchell. "'The Arguments I Seem to Hear': Argument and Irony in the *Crito.*" *Phronesis* 41, no. 2 (1996): 121–37.

Morrow, Glenn R. *Plato's Cretan City: A Historical Interpretation of the Laws.* Princeton, N.J.: Princeton University Press, 1960.

Munn, Mark. *The School of History: Athens in the Age of Socrates.* Berkeley: University of California Press, 2003.

Naddaf, Gerard. "Translator's Introduction." In Brisson, *Plato the Myth Maker,* vii–liii.

Nagy, Gregory. *Greek Mythology and Poetics.* Ithaca, N.Y.: Cornell University Press, 1992.

Nagy, Gregory. *The Best of the Achaeans: Concepts of the Hero in Archaic Greek Poetry.* Rev. ed. Baltimore: Johns Hopkins University Press, 1999.

Nagy, Gregory. *Plato's Rhapsody and Homer's Music: The Poetics of the Panathenaic Festival in Classical Athens.* Cambridge, Mass.: Harvard University Press, 2002.

Nettleship, Richard Lewis. *The Theory of Education in the Republic of Plato.* New York: Teachers College Press, 1968.

Nichols, Mary P. "Socrates' Contest with the Poets in Plato's *Symposium.*" *Political Theory* 32, no. 2 (April 2004): 186–206.

Nightingale, Andrea. "A Literary Interpretation of Plato's *Laws.*" *Classical Philology* 88, no. 4 (October 1993): 279–300.

Ophir, Adi. *Plato's Invisible Cities: Discourse and Power in the Republic.* Savage, Md.: Barnes and Noble, 1991.

Ovid. *Metamorphoses.* Translated by A. D. Melville. Notes by E. J. Kenney. Oxford: Oxford University Press, 2009.

Pangle, Thomas L. "The Political Psychology of Religion in Plato's *Laws.*" *American Political Science Review* 70, no. 4 (December 1976): 1059–77.

Parker, Holt N. "Sappho Schoolmistress." *Transactions and Proceedings of the American Philological Association* 123 (1993): 309–51.

Parker, Robert. *Athenian Religion: A History.* Oxford: Oxford University Press, 1996.

Pausanias. *Description of Greece.* 5 vols. Translated by W. H. S. Jones, H. A. Ormerod, and R. E. Wycherly. Cambridge, Mass.: Harvard University Press, 1918–39.

Pender, E. E. "Spiritual Pregnancy in Plato's *Symposium.*" *Classical Quarterly* 42, no. 1 (1992): 72–86.

Pfeijffer, Ilja Leonard. "Shifting Helen: An Interpretation of Sappho Fragment 16 (Voigt)." *Classical Quarterly* N.S. 50, no. 1 (2000): 1–6.

Pindar. *Carmina cum Fragmentis.* Edited by W. Christ. Leipzig, Germany: Teubner, 1953.

Pindar. *Epinicia.* Edited by Bruno Snell and Herwig Maehler. Leipzig, Germany: Teubner, 1987.

Planinc, Zdravko. *Plato Through Homer: Poetry and Philosophy in the Cosmological Dialogues.* Columbia: University of Missouri Press, 2003.

Plato. *Opera.* 5 vols. Edited by J. Burnett, E. A. Duke, W. E. Hickson, and W. S. M. Nicoll. Oxford: Clarendon Press, 1901–95.

Plato. *The Laws of Plato.* Translated by Thomas L. Pangle. Chicago: University of Chicago Press, 1980.

Plato. *The Republic of Plato.* Translated by Alan Bloom. New York: Basic Books, 1991.

Plutarch. *Lives* I. Translated and edited by Bernadotte Perrin. Cambridge, Mass.: Harvard University Press, 1914.

Plutarch. *Sayings of Spartan Women.* In *Plutarch's Moralia,* vol. 3, edited by F. C. Babbitt. Cambridge, Mass.: Harvard University Press, 1968.

Pseudo-Xenophon. "The Constitution of the Athenians." In *Aristotle and Xenophon on Democracy and Oligarchy,* translated by J. M. Moore. Berkeley: University of California Press, 2010, 19–61.

Recco, Gregory. *Athens Victorious: Democracy in Plato's Republic.* Lanham, Md.: Rowman and Littlefield, 2008.

Reeve, C. D. C. *Philosopher-Kings: The Argument of Plato's Republic.* Princeton, N.J.: Princeton University Press, 1988.

Rilke, Rainer Maria. "Archaic Torso of Apollo." Translated by Stephen Mitchell. In *The Selected Poetry of Rainer Maria Rilke.* New York: Vintage, 1989.

Roy, Jim. "The Threat from Piraeus." In *Kosmos: Essays in Order, Conflict and Community,* edited by Paul Cartledge, Paul Millet, and Sitta von Reden. Cambridge: Cambridge University Press, 1998, 191–202.

Russon, John. "Heidegger, Hegel and Ethnicity: The Ritual Basis of Self-Identity." *Southern Journal of Philosophy* 33, no. 4 (Winter 1995): 509–32.

Russon, John. "Hermeneutics and Plato's *Ion.*" *Clio* 24 (1995): 399–418.

Russon, John. "The (Childish) Nature of Soul in Plato's *Apology.*" In Fagan and Russon, *Reexamining Socrates in the "Apology,"* 191–208.

Russon, John, and John Sallis, eds. *Retracing the Platonic Text.* Evanston, Ill.: Northwestern University Press, 2000.

Sallis, John. *Being and Logos: Reading the Platonic Dialogues.* 3rd ed. Bloomington: Indiana University Press, 1996.

Sanday, Eric. "Philosophy as the Practice of Musical Inheritance: Book II of Plato's *Republic.*" *Epoche* 11, no. 2 (2007): 305–17.

Schindler, D. C. "Plato and the Problem of Love: On the Nature of Eros in the 'Symposium.'" *Apeiron* 40 (2007): 199–220.

Scolnicov, Samuel. *Plato's Metaphysics of Education.* London: Routledge, 1988.

Seaford, Richard. "Dionysus as Destroyer of the Household: Homer, Tragedy, and the Polis." In *Masks of Dionysus,* edited by Thomas H. Carpenter and Christopher A. Faraone. Ithaca, N.Y.: Cornell University Press, 1993, 115–46.

Seaford, Richard. *Reciprocity and Ritual: Homer and Tragedy in the Developing City-State.* Oxford: Oxford University Press, 1994.

Smith, Nicholas D. "Did Plato Write the *Alcibiades* I?" *Apeiron* 37 (2004): 93–108.

Sophocles. *Fabulae.* 2nd ed. Edited by Hugh Lloyd-Jones and Nigel Wilson. Oxford: Clarendon Press, 1990.

Stehle, Eva. *Performance and Gender in Ancient Greece.* Princeton, N.J.: Princeton University Press, 1997.

Thucydides. *History of the Peloponnesian War.* Translated by Rex Warner. Harmondsworth, U.K.: Penguin, 1972.

Tsiafakis, Despoina. "Life and Death at the Hands of a Siren." In *Studia Varia from the J. Paul Getty Museum,* edited by Marion True and Mary Louise Hart. Los Angeles: Getty Publications, 2001, 7–24.

Vernant, Jean-Pierre, and Pierre Vidal-Naquet. *Myth and Tragedy in Ancient Greece.* Translated by Janet Lloyd. New York: Zone Books, 1988.

Vlastos, Gregory. *Platonic Studies.* 2nd ed. Princeton, N.J.: Princeton University Press, 1981.

Weiss, Roslyn. *Socrates Dissatisfied: An Analysis of Plato's Crito.* Oxford: Oxford University Press, 1998.

White, F. C. "Love and Beauty in Plato's *Symposium.*" *Journal of Hellenic Studies* 109 (1989): 149–57.

Wohl, Victoria. "The Eros of Alcibiades." *Classical Antiquity* 18, no. 2 (October 1999): 349–85.

Woozley, A. D. *Law and Obedience: The Arguments of Plato's Crito.* London: Duckworth, 1979.

Xenophon. *Constitution of the Lakedaimonians.* In *Scripta Minora,* edited by E. C. Marchant. Cambridge, Mass.: Harvard University Press, 1962.

Zeitlin, Irving M. *Plato's Vision: The Classical Origins of Social and Political Thought.* Englewood Cliffs, N.J.: Prentice Hall, 1993.

Zuckert, Catherine H. "Becoming Socrates." In Fagan and Russon, *Reexamining Socrates in the* "Apology," 209–49.

Zuckert, Catherine H. *Plato's Philosophers: The Coherence of the Dialogues.* Chicago: University of Chicago Press, 2009.

INDEX

Achilleus, xvii, 28, 32, 53, 90, 94, 97, 98, 99, 100, 101, 117n27, 129n8
action, xiii, 9, 10, 30, 31, 35, 41, 103
active presence. *See* living presence
activity. *See* action
Aeschylus: *Seven Against Thebes,* 92
Agamemnon, 55, 90, 91, 98, 99, 100, 101, 129n5, 129n8
Agathon, xiv
agogē, 62
agriculture, 65, 66, 67
aidōs, 23, 25, 121n5, 123n38
Alcibiades (beloved): education of, 6–10; on learning, 6–10, 15; self-sufficiency of, 15–16
Alcibiades (Plato), xiv, 5–19, 114n15; authenticity of, 5; conversation of, 5–7; pederasty in, xvi, 5–19
Alcinous (king of the Phaeacians), 25, 68, 70
ameibō, 26
anelenktos, 127n5
Antigone (Sophocles), 123n36
Aphrodite, 24, 29, 115n7, 119n49
Apollo, 53, 65, 71, 73, 84, 85–86, 90, 91, 127n3
Apology (Plato), xiii, xvii, 8, 81–95, 113n4, 117n32; genre of storytelling, 94–95; Oedipus story and, 82–90, 92–93
aretē (excellence), xvi, 13, 19, 33, 43, 117n33
art, xiii, 49, 67, 71, 116n21
Athens, xiv, 72, 84, 104; Athenian culture, 9–10, 108; as cosmopolitan, 130n20; culture sharing, 11–12; death of Socrates and, 104, 128–29n20; democracy and, 37, 93–94, 95, 123n35, 128n16; eros as challenge to tradition, 18–19; family and, 18,

113n6; fleet, xiv; *polis* heroes, 87, 90; reverence for land, 124–25n3; shared spaces of, 9; typical narratives, 10–11
Attica, 67, 124n3, 126n24
authority, 49–57, 89
authorship, 5, 113n1
autobiography, 95

Bacchae (Euripedes), 74–75
Baracchi, Claudia, 122n30
beauty, desire of, 21, 33, 43, 117n29
beloved. *See erōmenos*
Bendis (Thracian god), xiv
body, love of, 17, 21

Cadmus myth, 60, 121n27, 122n32, 124n42
Calame, Claude, 53
care, 21, 22–28, 35. *See also* love; *philia;* correction and, 26; memory and, 26–27, 33; reading with care, 28–30; reciprocity and, 23; of self, 43
castration, 10, 18
Catalog of Ships, 54–55
Cephalus, xiv
Chairephon, 85
chorēgos, 53, 54
chorus, 18, 53, 54, 73, 93, 118n42, 126n20
Cicones, 70
Circe, 49, 55
citizenship, 66; change and, 122n30; *palimbola* (unstable habits), 66; terrain and, 66; tyranny and, 71
city. *See* polis
Cleinias, 18, 65, 66, 71
communicative act, 29
competence, 5–7

137